Here I Thought I Was Normal
Micro Memoirs of Mischief

By Frank Rocco Satullo

ZoneFree Publishing

Dedicated to
Rebecca, Cara and Dominic
Mom, Dad and Linda

Acknowledgements
Thank you to all who read these stories as I wrote and shared them privately to be sure that they are indeed not just my memoirs but validated by others. Although these are true stories, many names were changed to protect the innocent from potential embarrassment. Special thanks to Rebecca Satullo, Kathleen Satullo, Sandy Satullo, Linda Satullo, Cara Satullo, Dominic Satullo, Mara Cox, Matt Ackerman, Scott Hosier and Michael DeGiuseppe. Eric Kaswell (R.I.P.)

Here I Thought I Was Normal: Micro Memoirs of Mischief
Copyright © 2013 by Frank Rocco Satullo
Published by ZoneFree Publishing in Middletown, Ohio

ISBN 978-09724030-1-6
Printed in the United States of America

Cover design by Michael A. DeGiuseppe
Cover photograph by Scott Hosier

ZoneFree Publishing
6358 Castle Hill Dr., Suite #210
Middletown, OH 45044
513-207-6690
www.OhioTraveler.com

Contents

Introduction

By the time I was in my early twenties, people said I should write a book because I had already experienced more than many people do in a lifetime. Now well past my twenties, I wrote quick reads to share with family and friends about the past. They shared these stories with others and then feedback started leaking back to me by strangers. They enjoyed my stories, even though they didn't know me, because they identified with much of what I had experienced. In a way, my stories were their stories – mostly. Not only that, they said the micro-reads were wild, funny and touching. Who hasn't had such moments in life? I will admit, perhaps I have had more adventures than the norm and some crossed the lines beyond others' comfort.

CHAPTER 1:
THE MISCHIEVOUS YEARS OF YOUTH

Hand Caught in the Cookie Jar

My life of mischief began in a sandbox with a friend, Eddie. At least it's the first adventure I can remember.

It was an early summer morning and we wanted cookies but my mom said, "No."

I knew of another friend, Kyle, down the street and his mom always had a full cookie jar in her kitchen. So Eddie and I were off to get our fix even though I knew Kyle was at his dad's.

The house was locked and nobody was awake so we did the natural thing and slid through the doggy door. We were little tykes so we staggered the kitchen counter drawers to use as climbing steps.

I was on the counter, hand in the cookie jar, when Ms. E. appeared as a silhouette down the hall leading to the kitchen, "Rocky, is that you?"

My middle name is Rocco. I was named after a saint.

Ms. E. rubbed her eyes in utter disbelief as if she were still dreaming. The next thing she saw was two tiny butts squeezing through that doggy door, simultaneously.

Minutes later my mom stepped outside to see us in my sandbox and asked, dumbfounded, "Were you in Ms. E's house just now?"

Tasting chocolate chip on the corner of my mouth, I licked it and then said, "No."

Taking Candy from a Stranger

It was a very unusual day "down at the house," which is how everyone referred to my grandparents' place in Cleveland. If it were Sunday, there would be about 20 people there. But this was Saturday.

Grandpa must have been taking a nap because he and his vicious poodle were nowhere to be found. Grandma was where she always was, the kitchen. My parents set me up with my Batman and Robin coloring book in the living room and said they'd be back. If I needed anything, let Grandma know.

I kissed them goodbye, opened my book and colored. I got lost in what I was doing and never heard the strangers come inside. When I heard my name, I turned to look. I had been on my knees using the couch as a table to hold my coloring book.

"They're going to take you out for some candy," Grandma said, calmly.

I panicked. Scared stiff, fear consumed my entire body. Who were these people? I don't ever recall seeing them.

"Don't worry, this is your uncle," Grandma said, noticing my hesitation.

My dad came from a family of eleven. This was a younger brother of his. Maybe this sibling had been away or maybe he was busy doing other things or maybe I just never noticed him before. The big ole house could get pretty crowded and I'd be out playing with my cousins most of the time.

I wanted to cry for help, but instead went quietly with my captors.

My dad and his brothers and sisters grew up in two eras – the greasers listening to Motown and the long-haired freaky people who didn't listen to Motown. This was the early 1970's and this uncle character looked an awful lot like a guy they had statues and pictures of all over my church. He and his lady friend were all smiles, trying to make me feel comfortable. I wasn't.

They put me in the enormous backseat of their car. My feet only came to the edge of the seat I was sitting on. I didn't have to wear a seatbelt so I positioned myself in the middle so I could see the windshield between the front seats. I never said a word. Try as they might to get me to say something – anything, I wasn't talking. I just stared at them. I think it made them uncomfortable.

Better than candy, they thought, was ice-cream. That was sure to win me over. But I just ate mine and never even said thank you. They looked unhappy. This was not how they had planned for it to go, I could tell.

They took me back to Grandma.

I walked in, past Grandma and went straight to my coloring book and resumed a position as if I had never budged from the couch. I did not turn around again until my parents got me.

On the drive home, I broke a silent spell by saying, "I took candy from strangers today."

Runaway

Three houses down; that was the length of my leash on a bicycle.

I was a beginner and loving the freedom my new wheels gave me. Our street didn't have sidewalks, at least not down by my house. Still, it was safe.

The third house was approaching. I was on the edge of the road traveling opposite traffic. A car was coming from behind me as I turned into the middle of the road. I was startled when the driver beeped at me. Not a hello beep but an angry one.

Back home, I came to a stop against the side steps. This was the only way I could end a bike ride without crashing to stop. We had a long driveway. Mom was outside and I was about to go in for a glass of water when a police car pulled all the way up to the house. This was an incredible sight for me. The officer spoke with my mom and I didn't quite understand what it was all about. Finally, he approached me. Mom just stood off to the side.

Mesmerized by the uniform, holster and all, I didn't pay one bit of attention to a word he said. But I caught the gist. It was a lecture about bicycling safety. I was intimidated to say the least. In my mind, when you do something wrong and the police come, there's but one conclusion – jail!

"I have to go to the bathroom," I squeaked out.

The officer paused, looked at my mom and she said to be quick.

I was quick all right. I sprinted to my bedroom, grabbed underwear, a shirt, my favorite stuffed animal (a monkey) and then found a towel in the bathroom in which to wrap it all up. I only had cartoons and kids' shows as a guide, so in lieu of a stick to tie it to, I improvised and used a yard stick. I slipped out another door and was headed for the woods when my mom saw me.

"What are you doing? Where are you going?"

When I stopped and turned, the yardstick snapped and my sack flung to the ground.

Now I really did have to use the bathroom.

Instead, I had to listen to the rest of the safety lecture and then got the bonus lecture on running away. It all seemed so threatening to me. As the black and white pulled out of the driveway, I remember being very surprised that I wasn't in cuffs in the backseat.

After my bust I felt on the lam, always looking over my shoulder.

Brownies

I looked up from my chair, which was attached to my desk, and wondered if I had heard my teacher correctly.

Yep! She said it again – "…brownies!"

I put my pencil down from doodling on the desktop and refocused on the classroom.

"…So if you want to stay after school tomorrow for brownies, you'll need a note from your parents," she concluded at the bell.

When I got home, I promptly remembered to relay the information to my mom. She didn't bat an eye, wrote a quick note and tucked it inside my folder for tomorrow.

At the end of the next day, my mouth was watering. I gazed at the clock three times and all three times the long minute hand didn't budge. One minute to go and it seemed to take an hour.

Then, finally, brownie time!

"If you're staying after for brownies, line up here," my teacher directed.

Bam! I was second in line, eagerly waiting to satisfy my sweet tooth. My focus slowly turned foggy as background noise penetrated my one-track mind. It was laughter.

"Rocky wants to join the Brownies, Rocky wants to join the Brownies ..." was the chant gaining volume around me.

I looked around. I was the only boy in line. My teacher looked at me with an expression of ...unease.

"Rocky, boys can't join the Brownies. Brownies are Girl Scouts."

Free Money

Our moms were shopping together at the mall. Eddie and I were tired and didn't want to go into another store so our moms said we could wait by the fountain. We sat and stared at the water.

"Look at all that money," I said.

"People just give it away so I think, if we wanted, we could just take it," said Eddie.

"I don't know. Something doesn't sound right about that," I contemplated the options.

"It's just going to sit there forever so why not use it?" Eddie wondered out loud.

We looked around, rolled up our sleeves and stretched as far as our bodies could go without getting wet. That is, except for the rolled up sleeves pushed way up by our biceps. We raked in some coins, cupped them in our hands to show each other and see who had the bigger score. We smiled, looked around, shrugged and went fishing again. Before long, it just made sense to kick off our shoes, roll up our plaid pants and wade in to get that which we couldn't reach. Nobody said or did a thing. Granted, it was not crowded. Once we had filled every pocket we had, we put our shoes back on and stood looking at each other.

Instinct kicked in and we decided to flee the scene and fetch our moms. We casually squeaked away. Standing in the doorway of the last store we knew they had entered, we got on tippy toes and looked but could not find them. When we turned to exit, a security guard was in our way.

"Boys, boys, boys, what are we going to do here?" the guard said with what was a straight face. Although something seemed off, like he wanted to smile but couldn't.

"We didn't do anything, sir, except take some of that free money out of the fountain," I said.

"Oh, is that all?" he said back, looking down at our clothes.

Water was dripping from our saturated pants' pockets that bulged with our wet money.

"That's considered stealing. The mall owns that. You'll have to put it back," the guard continued.

So, we left a puddle where we had been standing and a trail of water across the hard mall floor back to the fountain. Later, maintenance was on the scene drying our path.

Instead of dumping the money back into the fountain, we tossed one coin at a time, making wishes.

About ten minutes later, our moms showed up, suspiciously looking at us and looking around.

Slowly and uncertainly, they mouthed the words, "Why are you so wet? And where did you get all of those coins?"

The Gift that Took

There was one gift I couldn't wait to play with after my birthday party. It was the metal tool box with real tools inside, albeit kid-size.

I opened the latch and lifted the lid to a world of possibility. I thought to myself, which tool should I use first?

Dad always had projects going on but he wasn't home. He worked half days on Saturdays. It sure would be nice to work next to the old man on something but I was too impatient to wait for him. I pulled out the hand saw. It was the largest thing in my new tool kit. I ran my finger along the saw blade to see how sharp it was. It pricked so I quickly pulled my finger away thinking I drew blood but I didn't. Holding the saw up, I examined it while thinking of what I could cut with it.

I went to our driveway next to our house and looked high into a majestic oak tree. The trees in our neighborhood towered over the houses. I walked back inside where Mom was still cleaning up from my party.

"Can I cut down a tree?" I asked, knowing what the answer would be but figured it was worth a try.

"Oh sure honey, have fun," Mom said to my amazement.

She knew me better than I knew myself. She knew what I had in mind and she was right. I went straight to the majestic oak tree and started ripping that saw blade across the thick, rough bark. My leverage was wrong so I abandoned the slight scrape – hardly even a groove – that I had started with 20 or more forward and backward motions. I took off my shirt like a real man, dabbed the sweat off my dripping face and went at it again, but lower this time. I kept at it, alternating my arms until both felt like they'd fall off.

Sitting against the tree trunk, defeated, I looked across the driveway at our house. I rationalized, if I get this sucker down, it might crush our home. I couldn't risk it.

I went inside and asked for lemonade. Mom mixed me up some, fresh.

"How's the tree coming along?" she asked.

Chugging the entire cup down in one, long, pulsating gulp, I tossed the empty into the sink and said, "Fine."

The cup was still rattling around the metal sink bottom when I hit the door. I was refreshed and ready to conquer.

This time, I picked on something more my size – the crabapple tree I remembered Dad planting a year or so earlier. I could have gone for the younger, flowering tree he planted just that spring but the older tree posed more of a challenge and, therefore, would be more of a triumph when I toppled it. Anyway, it met my new criteria of being tall enough to be worthy but not too thick to saw through it.

I cleaned the caked saw dust from my new saw blade with one of the old rags Dad kept in the garage. When the saw shined new again, I tossed the rag inside my tool kit just like I had seen my Dad do. Then I went to work.

Oh I felt good! I felt real good. I was cutting through this trunk with ease. The smell of victory burned each time I sawed into the wood. I gained strength and rhythm. As I neared the halfway point, a grin spread across my determined little face, ear-to-ear, anticipating...

"OH MY GOD! ROCKY! STOP!"

Mom flew from the front steps into the yard, screaming hysterically.

I dropped my saw and stepped back, "You said I could, you said I could, you said I could..."

The Gift of Not Receiving

It was a spring party at my grandparents' house in Cleveland's West Park area. This was my mom's side of the family.

Grandpa was beaming, ready to hand his two oldest grandsons surprise gifts. One gift was a kite and the other one was a...

Nobody remembers because we both wanted the kite!

My grandparents were working class folks who had happiness that money can't buy. But Grandpa's happy face quickly mangled into shock, confusion and then horror as my cousin and I battled back and forth with dueling words of "I want it – No, I want it!"

It was a noisy and crowded room but my dad must have noticed the hurt in my grandpa's wordless expression.

Dad leaned over and whispered to me, "Smile, take the other toy and say thank you."

I looked away from the kite and up to Dad with a facial plea to reconsider but in an instant I saw, clearly, *it was the right thing to do*. I promptly complied. As soon as I did, relief spread across Grandpa's face and suddenly I was happier than the kite would have made me. At least that's what I told myself.

Dad always helped people out. He basically knew everything about a home, landscaping, animals, plants, astronomy, you name it. I don't know what he had done for Grandpa this time but Grandpa was very appreciative and offered my dad money while we were piling into the car to go home.

"No-no, I can't accept that," Dad said, clasping his hands behind his back when Grandpa tried to hand him a wad of cash.

"I insist," Grandpa said.

"I just can't," Dad replied, shutting the back car door. I looked out the window intrigued by this benevolence Dad was displaying. First the kite, now cash, why does he turn away such great things, I wondered.

"Come on Sandy, just take it."

"No Cliff, I'm just happy to help." Dad got in the car, waved and said, "Goodbye."

As we backed into the street, Grandma Joan was on the front steps making her signature "peace sign" wave goodbye that we would come to love as we all grew older.

Dad's refusal to accept reward for good deeds left a strong impression on me.

Not long after, we were visiting my other grandparents at their home in a neighborhood near Cleveland's Edgewater Park. Dad's family was huge and many people visited weekly but we must have been the first ones there on this particular Sunday.

I sat on the couch across the room from Grandpa Frank. He got up from his chair, something I rarely saw him leave, and walked toward me holding out a silver dollar. He smiled as he handed it out for me to take.

"No-no-that's okay, Grandpa," I said shaking my head.

He briefly held the same confused look my other grandpa had over the kite incident.

After the pause, he took a step closer, leaned in and held the silver dollar out to me nodding that it's okay and said, "Take it."

I smiled and slid my hands back a little on the couch and said, "That's okay Grandpa, you keep it."

"Whattaya think I am some stranger off the street!" He was upset and I didn't know why.

The only thing I knew was that I was hurting his feelings by not taking it so I reached out, took it, smiled and said, "Thank you."

I could tell the moment for him was ruined. He sat back down and my dad walked into the room and sat next to me. Everyone was silent for a while.

For the longest time, I didn't understand when to accept things or not.

The "F" Bomb

Growing up, I don't ever recall my parents using the "F" word. They would sometimes cuss but the "F" word was never uttered.

That said, it's only a matter of time before you're exposed to it somewhere.

My introduction to the "F" word was at an uncle's house. It was one of those regular get-togethers we had with my dad's side of the family. He had enough siblings to suit up nearly TWO basketball teams and I had enough cousins to suit up nearly TWO football teams.

The adults would play games and joke around. The kids would disappear into the basement and have good times of their own. Kids being kids, when you learn something new, you can't wait to share it. Well, one of my cousins learned a new vocabulary word. So the fun during this visit centered on this word that rolled off the tongue with ease. And it was always delivered with a smile. So our introduction was without context other than sheer fun. We ran around using it liberally on each other all night long.

"You're a little f---er." *Giggle.*

"Ya, well you're a big f---er." *Giggle-giggle.*

"Get over here f---er." …"Make me f---er." …"What a bunch of f---ers." *Giggle-giggle-giggle!*

F---er this and f---er that, all night long. The word just brought joy to us all. We'd drop "F" bombs left and right – always with a huge smile or cackle of laughter.

I had never in my life been called a f---er so much and enjoyed every minute of it.

By the end of the night, as with most of these visits, we ran out of gas and ended up under blankets watching television. Bodies were strewn across the basement floor. Eventually, my parents came down to wake me and my sister to get in the cold car for the drive home.

We were on the highway cutting through rural Lorain County. All was quiet even though I was wide awake due to the cold. The heat had not yet reached me from the front vents.

"Hey Dad."

"What?" he answered while driving half asleep.

"YOU'RE A FUCKER!"

It's a good thing there was no one else on the highway at that hour because the car swerved from one lane to another as if someone hit the old man in the head with a two by four. Then, he craned his neck to shoot a look back at me and the car swerved again. I could see in his face that he was trying to figure out what to do next. I knew none of the prospects bode well for me.

Mom kept crying out, "He can't possibly know what that means, he can't possibly know what that means, he can't possibly know what that means."

The car recovered but I don't think Mom and Dad did.

Boyhood Crushes

I was interested in girls from the word go.

In first grade, I let Denise and Beth know it. But with that information, none of us knew what to do with it. In about third grade, our teacher put up "mail boxes" for each kid in the class. I competed in a love letter contest to win Mary's heart against my number one nemesis. He won.

True to my young spirit and knack for adventure, my first kiss was with my babysitter's daughter in my backyard pool – underwater! We thought that was so cool. Later, she stole my milk money before school. She made some sort of game with cardboard, coaxed me to insert my coin and voila – there it wasn't!

Also, I had the *hots* for my teacher. She was young, single and had long flowing platinum blonde hair. I even rode my bike to her window to give her an ice cream cone after school one spring day. Although I zipped from the store to the school as fast as I could, riding one-handed, the cone was soggy from half melted ice cream by the time I got there. She took it through the roll out window, smiled and said thank you. I was delighted. Ironically, I think that was the only parent-teacher conference my dad ever went to. He just wanted to see what this was all about, the crush not the grades.

My biggest boyhood crush was for the high school girl who lived kitty-corner from my house. She had a gymnast pole anchored between two huge trees. She'd flip and twirl on that thing for hours. I would watch from my front steps. I was still in grade school.

The high school bus stop was just a few houses down from mine. My mom had to drop me and my sister at a babysitter so we drove by it every morning. Waiting for the bus was the high school girl I had a crush on and her girlfriends. Sometimes,

I wedged a handwritten love letter through a cracked window as we drove past. She picked it up every time. I could see her and her friends giggling until they faded out of view from my back window.

My friend Eddie joined in my love letter campaign that summer. We began to irritate the high school girl. We would walk down a side street, sneak behind houses and around the side of hers to where she was sunbathing. Sometimes she was facedown without her top on. That drove us nuts. Like two rambunctious boys, we darted out of nowhere, dropped letters on her body as we cruised by – startling the hell out of her – and sprinted back to my house. It was a game we loved playing with her but at some point, she had had enough. The line was drawn right after our sinister plot of splashing her with a bucket of cold water to see if she'd jump up, topless, failed.

She offered a pact. One kiss and we leave her alone – forever! She was dead serious. It was a deal. We knew this was the end but hey, with a kiss, we could dream from that day forward. Eddie and I approached the side door of her house. We saw her brother peeking out a window. Eddie got embarrassed and ran away. I just clumsily flung myself into the garage door right there but I wasn't leaving – no way.

She came down the side steps in her shirt tied in a knot in the front showing off her bellybutton. I fell into a trance. She reiterated the conditions of the deal, making sure I was clear on things moving forward. I assured her my word was my bond and it was. Then, she leaned forward and down from the bottom step as I looked up and closed my eyes. I totally expected a kiss on the cheek which I would have been delighted with but she planted one directly on my lips. And it was everything I thought it would be. When I finally opened my eyes, head still in the clouds, I floated home.

By the end of summer, the deal was still a deal. I honored it.

Our cat had a litter of kittens and sometimes I'd play with them in the front yard. It was evening and I didn't have the kittens. I was just lying back in the grass anyway. The high school girl came over because she thought I had the kittens out. She was with her boyfriend. She sat close to me in the grass and asked how my summer was going. Her boyfriend seemed to not want to be there. I know I didn't want him there. I had pointed responses to her questions, trying to play cool. She got the message and left.

The guy looked back at me so I stuck my tongue out.

I was offended when he stuck his tongue back at me.

Bulldozing Paradise

My parents moved to Avon Lake before even the highway stretched that far west from the city. Over the years, it slowly evolved from a farm community to a full-fledged suburb.

The first sign I ever saw that one day the woods would be cleared and farms would be paved was when my neighbor friend, Jacob, and I stumbled upon a tractor at the edge of our blueberry spot in the woods behind where we lived. Our blueberry spot was pretty much a secret. My family used to go back there, regularly, and pick until we filled one or two buckets each, Dad had four. The blueberries came in all sizes. Our freezer was crammed with plastic bags-full all winter long. Mom made plenty of blueberry pies. My sister and I later turned picking blueberries into a business. We picked fresh blueberries for Mom's boss and co-workers. We even sold some to a nearby orchard so they could resell them.

Our woods were a paradise. Often, I woke up in the summer when Dad was leaving for work, which was around 5:30 a.m. He had to drive to Cleveland. Sometimes, I went downstairs when he was still there. It always seemed to surprise him. But once he left, I left too. I'd run to a friend's house and we'd go back to the creek to catch crayfish or just explore deeper reaches of the woods. We'd only come home when called.

Our mothers used to stand on the back steps and holler at the top of their lungs something like, "Ro-o-o-ockyyyy – suppertime!"

Voices carried far, echoing off trees and over open fields until we stopped, shushed each other and listened carefully for the second call to see whose mom it was.

Waking up to see the sunrise allowed for about six hours of uninterrupted time to do what we wanted and go where we wanted, no questions asked.

On this morning, we decided to hit a different stretch of creek than normal so we cut through the blueberry fields. And there it was; a backhoe-loader.

Of course, we climbed all over it, got in the driver's seat and pretended to plow things over. Almost without warning, Jacob started it and smoke gurgled from the pipe right in front of my face. We were moving.

We were in a state of pure joy motoring deeper into the field, laughing all the way. It was surreal — until we wanted to stop. For some reason, Jacob couldn't turn it off. We panicked. The machine slowly marched on. We watched the machine smash over brush, a wall of blueberry bushes, and it was headed for a tree line and just beyond that was the creek. I wanted to jump out.

Jacob messed around with some controls and I gave a play-by-play of things we were running over. He only looked up when we made a severe roll downward and then back up as the terrain turned wavy due to an old grape vineyard that used to stretch across the land.

About 20 feet from the trees and creek, Jacob brought the tractor to a complete stop and turned it off. We sat there like two farmers on a break, legs kicked up, laughing our nerves back to normal. What was most comical to us was the long path we made with the tractor through …everything.

"Imagine when the workers come to find the tractor way out here," I said.

We laughed and laughed at the thought of it.

Then, the imagery in our heads appeared before our eyes. There they were, far away but you could tell they were not happy.

We casually jumped down from the tractor, waved bye and disappeared into our shrinking paradise.

Grocery Store Playground

The creek was long and on one side it had rolling hills. Shaped like three sides of a square, we'd pick it up at a corner where our trail led. There was nothing but a mile or so of woods between our backyards and this "playground."

One day, we followed the creek up around another of its bends. Next to the grocery store was the American Legion. This was the time of year they would have live fire shooting ranges – turkey shoots I think they used to call them. I imagine if you missed the target, the round ended up in the woods. They weren't shooting so we didn't have to get our feet muddy in the creek. The creek on this stretch had no hills but its earthen walls were steep, camouflaged by bushes and saplings.

We decided to venture up to the grocery store. Men were at the dock unloading huge sides of beef. Out of the truck, they would slide one slab at a time down a cable attached to a hook. It would slam into the other slabs at the end of the tilted line. We sat on the concrete ledge and whooped it up when a good slam could be heard. We went nuts when meat parts flung off. The workers were grinning as they worked, letting us carry on.

When they were done, they took a break so we slipped inside to see what happened next. The saw noise was deafening so when a guy yelled at us we only saw lips moving. We exited at the nearest door and were now inside the store by the meat department and a water fountain. We strategically hit an assortment of free sample tables and actually satisfied our hunger.

Eddie suggested we play hide-and-seek. The game had never been this much fun. After a while, we decided on one more round. Then, we'd go back to the creek and woods.

I found the perfect spot. It was the cereal section. I moved enough boxes to slide my body behind an outer wall of cereal. Then, I pulled one box over to hide my face. I was so proud of my creativity. I knew I'd never be found.

About the time I was cramping and dozing off, I thought about ditching my spot to see what everyone else was up to. That's when I heard someone closing in. They were onto me. They must have been. Box after box was being moved to see what was behind it, I presumed. My anxiety from the anticipation of being found was off the charts high.

That last box I placed in front of my face was moved. I looked out and saw the slacks of a lady. She was holding the box between us. It looked like she was reading the back of it because staring at me was Count Chocola. I held my breath and remained motionless. I don't know when she sensed me but when she did, she dropped the Count and screamed so damn loud, I felt like bursting from my hideout and sprinting for the exit. But my body would not move.

In the manager's office, I got a good scolding but before he was finished, someone came in and alerted him of more boys creating mischief.

He pointed at me and said, "Don't you move!"

He disappeared and so did I.

Cautiously, I walked out of the office, looked around, turned the corner and strolled right out the front doors. Once I was in the parking lot, I sprinted around the far corner of the building into an open field heading for the woods. I kicked into overdrive when my friends flew around the opposite corner of the building and into the field. Three men were in hot pursuit. We made a "V" toward each other and the creek.

We ran right up to the edge of the creek and jumped. We knew we couldn't clear it and that wasn't what we had in mind. We splat into the far bank, righted ourselves and splashed down the middle of the creek in the direction of the American Legion. The men weren't far behind. They drew closer quickly, running along the upper edge of the creek peering down when their view wasn't obstructed.

We stopped when they stopped.

Everyone took notice of the gunfire.

One of the men made a motion with his finger for us to come his way.

We looked at each other and bolted the other way to "safety."

School Roof

Eddie and I were bored now that we lost the last ball we owned. So, we did like any bored kids would do and climbed a tree.

The tree happened to be at our elementary school. Our bikes were in the grass below us.

"I wonder how many balls have been hit up on that roof during school recess?" I asked.

I don't know if you could see the "light bulbs" appear over our heads but we felt it.

We dropped out of the tree and approached the front of the school studying it. Without a word between us, I hoisted Eddie up. He had placed his foot in my clasped hands, palms up. With a good thrust, he grabbed onto the inside of the letter "o" in the word "school." He swung a leg and used leverage from another letter to twist his body higher and then onto the overhang of the front doors. Meanwhile, I managed to use a nearby window sill to maneuver to the letters, and with Eddie's outstretched hand I joined him on the overhang. It took teamwork but we scaled the building to the rooftop where we found a ladder anchored to a taller brick wall. It led to the highest rooftop – the gymnasium.

Jackpot!

We were so giddy we couldn't contain ourselves. We hooted and hollered and in retrospect, I'm sure our voices carried. We found baseballs, tennis balls, kick balls and even a football. It was Christmas in July.

Once we punted the last of the balls to the lot behind the school we surveyed our score and returned to the ladder, grinning.

"Oh no!" Eddie froze. "Cops!" he managed to blurt out even though it was just one.

The officer saw us.

"Get down here, NOW!" He yelled and we definitely heard, but we didn't listen.

Leaping without climbing all the way down that ladder to the main roof, we rolled to the opposite side of a pitched roof from the policeman's

28

location. Then we half-ran, hunched over, maneuvering odd obstacles from one end of the building to the other.

With no more rooftop ahead of us, we turned around and cautiously peered over the low-pitched peak of this wing of the building. To our surprise, the policeman was still looking up from the front door area far-far away from where we now perched. His peculiar body movements suggested he was not at all happy.

We made it. We actually made it.

We hang dropped from the end of the building. Eddie yelped in pain. He hurt his ankle so bad he couldn't put much pressure on it. So we made like Army men, using three legs and a shoulder to carry the wounded from the battlefield lickety-split. Once we arrived at the wood line, we looked back.

The coast was clear.

About an hour later, Eddie limping, we reached deep for the bravery that would take us back to the school to fetch our bikes.

They were gone!

Stolen?

Eventually, we had to go home for supper. But when I arrived home, my mom and dad "greeted" me. The bikes weren't stolen. They were taken by the policeman. You see, we used to have to register them at the police station and get a sticker license if you were a youth in our town back then. So, *Mr. Policeman* ran the tags and we were busted!

I sat at the station much like a cops and robbers TV show. Looking back, I'm sure my mom and dad must have been laughing behind glass. I was in a chair, knees nearly touching the officer's knees.

There was no table, just two chairs and yes, a bright light in my face. He was spitting mad, leaning in, drilling me, lecturing me, showering me in lip spray as his mouth smacked open and closed.

I never spoke a word – just stared. I was scared.

When we left, Eddie was getting buzzed through the jailhouse door with his mom. He was already crying.

Hurts So Good

Standing deep in the outfield grass at Sunset Park, I was bored.

It was my first year in little league baseball. I was young for my grade and small for my age. Most of the kids were one or two years older than I.

The coach called out to me, the lonely right fielder, "Catch this and practice is over. Miss it and you all run laps."

No pressure, right?

Damn, that ball was a towering pop-up. I could have run home, changed my underwear and returned in time to catch it. Instead, I stood there like the Statue of Liberty …waiting. When it fell closer, it grew in my eyes to the size of a softball, then a basketball and then …

It skimmed the outer leather of my glove and ripped my ear lobe. Do you know how much blood is in a nice juicy ear lobe like mine? I didn't either until that moment. I looked down for the ball and wondered why the entire left side of my shirt was red.

People were running, yelling, "Call an ambulance."

By the time I was brought from the outfield to the street, an ambulance was there but my parents weren't. So, they couldn't take me anywhere. I was treated on the spot, hearing every gasp from everybody that got close enough to see the blood, including two paramedics. When my parents arrived, I went to the hospital and got stitched up.

A few days later, I was eating lunch in the school cafeteria. We sat at long rows of tables, lunch monitors walking up and down the aisles like the Gestapo. I saw an older kid a few aisles over smack a ketchup bottle's plastic bottom down on the table forcing ketchup to shoot up making his friends laugh. The Gestapo didn't notice. Being a prankster, I did the same. Only, I really smacked that sucker hard! Ketchup shot nearly to the ceiling, but the cool thing was how it landed in a perfect line right down the middle of the table between lunch boxes. The line of splatter was so long, kids looked up, not knowing what just happened.

But the head of the Gestapo did!

The meanest lunch monitor marched at me with steam coming from her nostrils or so I imagined. She grabbed me by the ear – Yes! That ear – and dragged me to the office albeit I was on my feet trying to keep pace, pleading because of the pain.

She had no idea.

Standing before the principal in his office, she reported my misconduct but his God-awful expression made her stop and follow his line of sight right to my ear lobe pumping blood through the stitches.

She nearly fainted.

I caught on fast and clutched my ear, moaning, "Please stop hurting me."

Gemini

Back when the Gemini was new at Cedar Point Amusement Park, my coach took our entire little league baseball team.

I was borderline tall enough to ride roller coasters where-as most kids my age were veterans having beat the stick in height a year earlier.

It was a hot summer night, nearing closing time. I finally worked up the courage to ride the Gemini. At the time, Gemini was the tallest, fastest and steepest wooden roller coaster on the planet. It featured two rollercoasters that raced side-by-side.

My teammates knew I was a rookie about to ride my first real rollercoaster. So, they proceeded to tell me about the grisly death that happened earlier in the summer. Coincidentally, it was to a boy my age and size – barely big enough to ride. Of course, none of that happened but how was I to know. It seemed awfully convincing to me.

The dark got darker. The creaky wooden ride got creakier. The screams overhead turned blood-curdling. And the taunts were unceasing. The boys knew they had me on the ropes. I was not easy to crack but they sensed I was cracking. They said I probably shouldn't ride. If they let me on, it may truly be a death-defying experience.

I felt smothered and vulnerable as the line snaked its way closer to the pavilion. Fear consumed my mind and spread throughout my body. My friends were determined to drive this home. The mission was to see me cry and I was close.

My eyes welled up. The levy was about to break. Then ...

"That is e-nough!" sounded the voice of a guardian angel.

I turned to see the prettiest woman I had ever laid eyes on in my young life. Then her hand cradled the back of my head and drew me in. Before I could do anything, my face was nestled perfectly between her D-cups.

She lightly scolded my buddies. I really don't know what she said because my hearing was muffled. The time I spent with my head in the "clouds" was so long, I could barely breathe. I didn't care if I suffocated.

But all good things must come to an end. And I was released. She smiled big at me and said that everything they said was just to scare me – none of that happened. What she didn't realize was that by that time, I could care less. I was ready to take on the world.

I turned to face my friends with renewed bravado.

The oldest kid, and star pitcher on our team, pulled me aside to whisper how awesome it must have been to be me for the past few minutes. The rest of the team was in shock and awe, too. They treated me like their hero and thought I should play it up more to see if I could get a second round at second base.

When I refused, one by one, they started to whimper, "I'm scared to go on the ride," with one eye on the pretty woman hoping she would comfort them.

That night, I had experienced the most exhilarating thing in my young life, and the Gemini was a close second.

BB Gun

Christmas morning arrived. Mom let us open our stockings but Dad made us eat breakfast before getting to the presents under the tree. I already knew what I was getting. I found the stash deep in Mom's closet weeks ago. Although the presents had already been wrapped, I peeled the tape back and bent the paper just enough to see what was inside one and then moved on to another. I even knew what my sister was getting.

We always got a dozen or so presents each on Christmas, so I had to go through the motions with 11 of them just to get them out of the way so I could seize the only thing I was truly looking forward to getting – a BB gun!

I didn't anticipate having to compete with my dad for a turn to use it. He spent too long showing me how it's done.

"Daaaad! I get it. Now let me have a turn!"

"One more shot," he laughed, and then he took several more shots.

The fireplace was roaring, the sliding glass door was open, the backyard was covered in snow and I was a sniper …for about 10 minutes before Dad said we needed to close the door.

After all of the lectures, demonstrations and promises, I became the poster-child of why not to give a kid a BB gun.

At first, I was a good boy. I'd line bottles upside down along the back fence. When I shot them to pieces, I'd put the pieces on the fence and shoot them. As my targets got smaller, I got better. I learned how to adjust the sights above a target knowing the BB would arch over distance. I became a deadeye!

When I ran out of inanimate objects to shoot, I set my sights on a bird in a tree overlooking the neighbor's driveway. First shot and I ...missed it? I was too good to miss at that range. I put it back in my sights and just as I was about to squeeze the trigger, the bird fell upside down still clinging to the branch with his feet. I lowered my gun, stunned. The bird wouldn't fall. I knew I couldn't have a dead bird hanging upside down where the preacher would see it and surely raise hell. I spent the next 15 minutes shooting that poor thing full of holes until it fell – right in front of the preacher pulling in with his car!

That was the first time my BB gun was taken away.

When I got it back, I shot some more birds. One day, I grew impatient waiting for a target so I put bread out, sat in a lawn chair on the patio and plucked them off one-by-one until Dad pulled in. I nearly crapped my pants because there were bodies all over the backyard. I ran to the driveway to greet my dad and to walk him inside, thereby distracting him from looking out back as he walked out of the detached garage. I continued to escort him through the kitchen making sure he didn't look out the back windows. He went to his bedroom to change out of work clothes and I bolted out the back door to fling my prey into the woods.

I never did that again. It seemed too cruel. No sport in it. In fact, I never shot another bird after that. Instead, I'd get kicks by taking friends into my garage and shutting the door.

I'd say, "Cover your eyes."

Then, I'd pull the trigger and you could hear the BB ricochet all around us. It sure got the adrenaline pumping. I was amazed it never hit us — ever. I must have done this "trick" a dozen times.

BB guns became the rage in the neighborhood so we'd go play Army in the woods. We'd have forts and wars. Yep, we'd actually shoot each other. We wore shop goggles though — the plastic things that completely surrounded the eyes. These good times ended when I shot Denny. He went home and needed minor medical attention from his mom. He wasn't a good liar. First, he told a tale of some older kids chasing him, holding him and shooting him in the woods.

When the police showed up, he sang like a canary and said, "Rocky did it!"

That time the police confiscated my BB gun.

Stirring up a Hornets' Nest

We had been in position for 30 minutes, firing our BB guns at the hornets' nest.

It wasn't just any hornets' nest — it was the mother of all hornets' nests! Our BBs seemed to have no effect. We shifted our strategy to the base where it hung in the tree but we were just too far. Granted, it was a safe position when calculating how far the hornets were seen buzzing around the nest. However, we needed to get closer since our target went from a huge gray mass to the base where it clung to the tree branch.

Some of us dressed in green camouflage, others in white tee shirts, blue jeans and ball caps. We low crawled through the waist-high, light brown brush of the open field and found a new position much closer.

It was close enough to put the sling-shot into action with more accuracy.

"Wow! Nice shot!" was the consensus as the hole was visible and the flurry of hornets thickened.

Twenty minutes later, several holes torn into the nest, we realized this could take all day to bring it down. We needed a bolder plan.

"Manny, run up closer and throw this at it."

"Screw you!" was the reply.

"C'mon, man," the peer pressure poured on until Manny, the youngest of our group, went home.

Down a man, we re-examined the pecking order.

"Don't look at me, you go," Jacob said to Kyle.

"Heck no," said Kyle.

"Wussies!" I yelled as I sprinted in an arch pattern at the nest with a chunk of shale and whipped it like I was skipping a rock. It missed.

"Crap, I think I got stung," I said when my adrenaline level came back down as I returned to our position.

Like a dam giving way, the throbbing-stinging pain spread across my left hand. I tucked it into my gut, bending over.

"Who's the wussie now," said Eddie.

Jacob and Kyle laughed.

Meanwhile, I had spotted what looked to be a section of telephone pole on my loop back. We low crawled to it. Weird as it was, indeed, a small cut section of a telephone pole lay in the brush. It was the perfect size to get two of us on each side and have room to spare. Plus, it was light enough to …

"Ahh, this'll be awesome!"

"Did you fall and crack your head or something," they replied.

But when I really wanted to be persuasive, I could usually bring my friends around to doing the most stupid of stunts.

So there we were, rushing at a mega hornets' nest with what can only be described as a battering ram. We hit it solid, launching it straight into the ground where all hell broke loose.

We scattered, running for our lives, running for our homes – more to the point, our moms – screaming bloody murder the entire way.

At first, I was okay, running through the field. I laughed heartily seeing Jacob fall, get up and cry his eyes out he was getting stung so badly. Just when I thought I might have escaped unscathed, it felt like I was sprayed by tiny, potent bullets from a machine gun. From my fingers waiving frantically in the air, across my outstretched arms to my head, neck and shoulders, even down my back, butt and legs, I went from thinking this prank was hysterical to being hysterical.

I stumbled through my back gate, crying like there was no tomorrow.

Playboy Collection

Like any red-blooded American boy, I had a Playboy collection.

Well, it was actually a collection of all the classics; Hustler, Penthouse, Playboy, etc. Our corner store, Lawson's at the time, used to keep them on the magazine rack close to the door. The checkout was in the back of the store. Go figure.

Needless to say, we easily applied our "five-finger discount" and started a library in the woods. When it rained, we'd make another trip to the store. So it goes.

We were young – too young to do anything that might make us go blind.

Eventually, in the life of crime, you get comfortable and up the ante. So the magazines found a home in …my home. Well preserved, the stack grew. But so did my conscience. Maybe all that churchin was having an effect.

I tried to smuggle them out of the house a little at a time, under my shirt.

And for that, my mom noticed. "What are you doing?"

"Nothing."

But dozens were still upstairs. It ate at my brain.

Well past bedtime, I stood at the top of the stairs crying out to my parents, unable to endure this spot on my soul any longer, "Take them away! I don't want them anymore! I'm sorry."

Both of my parents ran upstairs. They had to think the situation serious for one to come to my aid but both?

I led them to my room and started shoveling piles of magazines at them, "Take them, take them all."

Their eyes bulged to the size of softballs.

They took them. Baffled and silent, they took them all.

Trombone Lessons

We gathered in the cafeteria of Eastview Elementary School for a demonstration of musical instruments.

I was completely uninterested until I heard the greatest sound – "BoooWaaamp!"

"What was that?" I asked, abruptly leaving my daydream and tuning in for the first time.

From the smile on his face, the person playing the instrument surely enjoyed it. How could he not? He took that long thing, the outer slide I think it's called, pushed it way out and quickly pulled it back in again to make music to my ears.

The minute I got home, I said, "Mom, I want to play trombone!"

I think my parents were shocked. They asked me a bazillion questions to make sure I was doing it for the right reasons. They wanted to make sure I'd stick with it. I didn't realize how much a trombone cost. After I said whatever it took to gain their approval, they signed me up and hunted for a bargain. I was delighted.

When I had that thing in my hands, sitting in my bedroom, I opened the important looking case and gazed at the shiny brass inside. I opened my window so I could let the world hear the great sounds I was about to breathe.

"GrrrbrrpUUrumphtphlagrr. Coufflurrrmphtba," belted out the upper window, echoing all around.

The heads of neighbors working in their yards turned, looking around, searching for the talent that was me. I knew I could serenade them and bring joy to their labor.

"GrrrbrrpUUrumphtphlagrr. Coufflurrrmphtba," I played over and over trying to master that sound that brought me to love the trombone.

"For crying out loud, shut your window!" ...It was Dad but I couldn't see him wherever he was outside.

My trombone lessons were at school. It was in the same tiny room I used to have speech therapy. I couldn't make the "TH" sound. Three was tree and so forth – or forf. But as I mastered that sound, so too would I master, "BoooWaaamp!"

I worked hard at my craft. I studied my music more than schoolwork. One day, some "fellow" players of musical instruments came a calling at my babysitter's house.

"Rocky, some girls want to play music with you in the front yard," said Mrs. Simpson.

"Tell them to go away, I'm not ready," I said, horrified.

I used to be shy. I suppose I've always had situational shyness.

They persisted so I agreed that if I could play from inside and they from outside, we'd have a compromise. And so it was …until I noticed I was the only one playing. I peeked out the window from behind a curtain. They were gone.

I had given this my best for nearly two weeks. It was time to face the music – I sucked!

I went into my lessons and tugged my teacher to the side and said I wanted to quit.

She said, "Now Rocky, we aren't allowed to let anyone give up until they've tried for at least six weeks (long pause and sigh) but in your case, I'll make an exception."

Playing with Matches

Like early man, we climbed down from the trees and discovered fire.

There was a place in the woods, not far back, that was like a hideout. It was surrounded by huge pine trees so dense it created seclusion from the outer world. You'd have to look very closely from the trail right next to it to even know it was there. Inside it was a huge open space. The ground inside was thick with pine needles.

We used to sneak books of matches taken from parents who still smoked at the time. In our hideout, we'd build stacks of pine needles and set it on fire. Just something about it captivated us. The curdling smoke, the burning needles, and the way it would start slow and grow when you piled more pine needles on top. We were very careful to snuff it out before abandoning the area. We'd even clear a perimeter of pine needles around it so no flames could unexpectedly spread.

This fascination grew and so did our creativity. We introduced little, plastic, green army men to the scene and pretended the stacks of pine needles were enemy huts in Vietnam. We would spend hours making strongholds and villages. A flick of a match here and there signified the firefights and in the end, the entire scene we built was torched. Some of the army men suffered injuries as was evident in the partially melted pieces. This was because they were heroes throwing themselves in harm's way to save innocent villagers.

Then, we did similar stuff with Star Wars figures. We'd hold the heads or shoulders of storm troopers close to the miniature fires we'd set to melt just the right amount. Then, we'd act out a battle and interchange normal storm troopers with the burned ones to show they had just been hit by a laser gun or light saber. Half of my Star Wars figures looked like they belonged to a burn ward at the hospital. I would hide them in a shoe box under the good ones when I'd go home so my parents wouldn't see.

The last fire we ever set was soon after school let out for the summer. We brought a bunch of school papers back to our hideout, started a fire and fed it steadily. The fire grew with every piece added to it. It was not the typical miniature fire we usually burned and put out. We had a pretty good blaze going. The problem with that is it created a lot of smoke. So, our preacher neighbor came to investigate. When we saw him trying to find a way to get in the natural fortress, we low crawled out a back tunnel-like exit and ran home.

The preacher put out the fire. Many of our papers were just half burned. Unfortunately, our names were on some of the unburned portions. To put it mildly, our parents poured cold water on our pyromania.

A while later, a couple of younger boys on the street had done exactly what we used to do. Maybe it's a part of boyhood. Theirs was the mother of all fires. It spread overnight in a slow, smoldering way through the open field and beyond, stretching behind half a dozen houses. Eventually the fire department had to bring fire trucks between two houses to hose everything down. For weeks, maybe months, afterward, if you walked into the charred field, ash smoke would still billow up with each step, emitting the smell of charred earth. Everything was blackened for the longest time.

So, we went back to climbing trees.

The Neighborhood Bully

"Tank" — like any bully — was lashing out at the world for his own unhappiness. You wouldn't know that back then. Growing up, there was nobody more feared in our neighborhood but, for better or worse, I stood up to him.

It all started with my new skateboard. A friend and I took it to a freshly repaved, asphalt street with a hill. Before long, Tank walked around the corner, ripped the board from my hands, went down the hill and flipped my new toy high overhead. Bam! It was chipped. I called after him and he flipped me off and went on his way.

Days later, he was riding a bike past my house and I made him stop. Mind you, he was a couple years older than me. Standing in his way, I confronted him about my damaged skateboard. He got off his bike, put me in a headlock and proceeded to beat me into oblivion. Unable to move, when the flurry of one-armed punches went from my face to my gut, I was able to cry out loud.

My mom heard and came to the front steps to see me getting beat up. She felt I was old enough that her interference would only make matters worse for me. So, as difficult as it was, she didn't break it up. Instead, she became my ring manager.

"Stop crying and start fighting!"

I couldn't believe my ears. I much preferred the embarrassment of mommy to the rescue over the current pain.

"You can't cry and fight at the same time," she continued.

The punches slowed.

Tank probably couldn't believe this was not being broken up. I think he pitied me.

Mom called out again.

Then Tank stopped, put me at arm's length and said, "You got it as bad as I do," and walked to his bike and left.

Then, behind closed doors, Mom gave me all the babying I needed.

Tank disappeared for a while. He spent a year or longer in the detention home.

After he got out, he rode his bike by my house and asked, "Hey Satullo, want to get your ass beat again?"

"Not unless you broke something of mine," I couldn't believe what just came out of my mouth.

He smiled and rode on.

That summer, at the neighborhood park, kids were wrestling on top of what we called the "green box." It was a large metal box with games, art supplies and sports equipment inside for summer park counselors to open and use with the kids. But it was lunchtime and the green box was closed. Tank rode his bike up and joined the game of king of the mountain atop the green box. Everyone was intimidated, me included. Tank was about to throw me off when something happened to his balance. I found my feet and flipped him over head first. He landed on his shoulder and broke a bone.

I saw my life flash before my eyes.

"Rock, you did this, help me."

So I did.

We ended up at his house and called an ambulance.

I don't remember seeing him again because he was always in and out of trouble going to kids' jail. He was never out long enough for our paths to cross.

At the beginning of a new quarter in high school, Tank walked into one of my classes. The teacher wasn't there when Tank made his grand entrance by planting a kid standing in his path butt first into a trash can. Then, he eyed up the rows of desks to find a place to sit. All eyes turned from his gaze.

He came up the row next to mine, stood by the seat next to mine, and told its occupant, "You're sitting in my chair."

That kid moved fast.

Tank sat down, stretched back low and cool and cocked his head toward me and asked, "Hey Rock, what's up?" like we were old friends.

Years later, I heard he had gotten into a knife fight in a nearby city and was stabbed to death by a gang.

Sticker Confessions

When I played Little League baseball, we raised money by selling stickers door-to-door. The whole town was basically carved up and each team was assigned various neighborhoods to canvass. We wore our uniforms, partnered up and tried to outdo our teammates because of the incentive awards for the most money raised.

My buddy, Bobby, and I were on a mission to win. We ran from house to house figuring speed was key. If someone didn't answer after the second knock, we slowly backed away allowing a few more seconds and then bolted for the next door. We had two hours before our coach would swing by to get us before dark.

Halfway through, we knew we were raking in the dough at record speed. Our enthusiasm gained more momentum after a generous donation. Once that deal was sealed, we sprinted to the next house, ignoring the driveway and sidewalk. Instead, we cut across the lawn and leaped the waist-high hedges, running to the next door.

Instead of a knocking sound, the glass on the "screen" door shattered. We paused for the first time in over an hour.

"Run!"

We skipped the next two houses and went to the third, figuring that would put us in the clear. We didn't know what to do so we continued to sell stickers. Resuming our duties, we kept gawking over our shoulders down the street to see if anyone noticed what we had done.

Minutes later, police arrived at the house we had damaged. Then, our coach caught up to us. There we were, time a ticking, having to explain ourselves to coach and the police.

We weren't permitted to continue on our selling spree, but the officer and coach believed what we did was truly an accident. Imagine our surprise when the officer said it wasn't our fault. It turned out that actual glass in a door like that was illegal. City ordinance or something only permitted Plexiglass – for obvious reasons I supposed.

We were in the clear and so were our parents as far as having to pay for damages. But the whole fiasco cost us time and therefore prizes. We didn't seem to mind by the time it was all said and done.

The next day at school, buzz circulated about how we smashed in someone's door. People made it sound like we were vandals. I resented that.

In all the hub-bub of the night before, I neglected to turn in my remaining stickers. I told a kid on the way home from school and he said I should try to sell them and pocket the money. I thought I'd give it a shot just to see if I could pull it off. However, it seemed too devious an act to go the whole nine yards and don my uniform. Therefore, I set out in just my ball cap and stickers.

People bought my stickers. I couldn't believe it.

Sure, there were folks who said, "You boys just came through here last night."

I was down to the last of my stickers by the time I made it through the neighborhood and ended up by a tiny old bar. I had never seen the inside of a bar so I walked in, thinking I had good reason. Right away they tried to shoo me out but I told them I was selling stickers to support my little league baseball team. The guy tending bar paused while patrons opened their wallets. Cash was tossed my way by the fistful.

One guy bellowed, "Hell, I don't even live here but how ya gonna tell this kid no – he's got some balls walkin' in here."

Another voice called out, "Hey, where's your uniform anyway?"

That night, I lay in my bed counting my money. I was happy I pulled off the unlikely but I couldn't sleep. My conscience began to plague me. I knew I had been dishonest. I deceived people and basically stole their money. I rolled out of bed, flicked on my desk lamp and wrote a note to go to Confession before church on Sunday.

At the next baseball practice, I gave the loot to my coach and said I forgot to turn it in. He didn't think anything of it.

Ambush!

My sister, Linda, was three years younger than I. We'd go from being best friends to fighting at the drop of a dime. So it goes for most siblings.

Very early in life, during a spat with my sister for taking a toy, I smacked her arm to make her drop it. Dad saw this and made it crystal clear that there was never a circumstance that made it okay to hit a girl – ever. That message stuck with me on my buttocks for hours and in my mind – always!

Still, as we grew older, that didn't mean I had to be seen with my "embarrassing" little sister. It cramped my style. When we walked to and from elementary school, I would make her walk about 20 feet ahead of me. I didn't realize until we were much older how much this upset her because she thought the world of me.

So it was with this rule of mine that we rode our bicycles home from a neighborhood store. Mom had given us some money to get ice cream cones, but I had to ride with my sister. On the way home, I made her speed up so she was several houses ahead of me. We took a side street we barely used. It had a stretch of houses and kids I didn't like to go past but Linda had a friend near the corner so we rode that way anyway.

As Linda rode past the stretch of houses, some of the kids I didn't like were playing out front. I saw one break from the lawn and run into the street at my little sister. She was innocently riding her bike, not even paying attention. The event unfolded before my eyes as if it were in slow motion. I couldn't believe what I just witnessed. The kid, a year older than I, who ran out, said my sister wasn't to ride down his street. His face grimaced in anger. My sister, scared, slowed down. That's when he planted a forceful punch square in the middle of her back as she tried to lean forward, barely pedaling.

I heard the thud. It was that loud. I must have made some sort of noise as I came barreling toward him on my bike. His body gyrated out of surprise and confusion. He was surprised because he had not seen me coming when he ran out and attacked my little sister for no reason. He was confused as to where to retreat because it was clear I was coming to kick his ass!

I leaped from my speeding bike and sprinted after him. He ran around to the back of his house, opened and closed the screen door behind him and locked it. When I got there, just steps behind, I smacked into the closed door, stopped and glared at him through the screen. He felt safe enough to make cocky faces at me and mouth off. He used cuss words and smirked the whole time.

There was no way this injustice was going unpunished in my mind. So, I did the unthinkable. I smashed through the screen door. Actually, I ripped the metal frame from the wall as I came through the screen. My adrenaline was in overdrive. His shock immobilized him. I knocked him down and pounded him furiously right there inside his home. Just like any neighborhood fight, kids came from everywhere to check it out. When I exited the house, laser eyed and bloody knuckled, people were unusually quiet as opposed to the mob-mentality cheers that usually accompanied such occasions.

I walked casually to the street, asked Linda if she was okay and rode bikes home, together.

Snow Shoveling

It was the day after a blizzard – time to make some scratch.

Just after breakfast, the gang received the relay call. Bundled up and raring to go, we hit the streets with our shovels. Door-to-door, we knocked out driveway after driveway at about five to ten bucks a pop.

We headed back to my house for warmth and lunch. On the way, we crossed paths with the competition. A snowball fight ensued.

The doorway pooled with the melted, dark, gray slush from our boots. Our socks hung in front of every heater we had in the kitchen, dining and family room. Grilled cheese and hot cocoa never tasted better.

Recuperated, we trudged out into the great white again, shovels over shoulders.

"No-no-no-YES-no-no-no thanks," pretty much summed up the afternoon.

It was approaching dinnertime and we were determined to get one more "yes" before calling it a day ...and before frost-bite set-in.

We ventured down a street we normally didn't travel on and found a nice long driveway still buried in fluff that was almost waist-high. This was a ten dollar job. The house was behind the garage, a peculiar set-up. A middle-aged woman opened the door. She gave us the creeps. Age had not been kind to her. But, she smiled, strangely, and said we could shovel her drive. We set the price and went to work.

This job nearly killed us. It was the deepest snow of the day because of a drift. It was also the tail end of our grueling labors. We were tired, aching and oh so cold! It was difficult to feel our fingers and toes. We were anxious to finish.

The apron of the driveway was particularly tough. The snow there was higher than the rest. Actually, it was more of a hardened sludge, compliments of the snow plow. We muscled our way through and collapsed on our backs when we finished.

It was time to get paid and go home. We were whipped but smiling.

We went around the garage to the front of the house. It took some determined knocking before the woman finally came to the door. She seemed angry at our incessant pounding but we weren't going anywhere, we knew she was home. In short, she snarled that she didn't know who the hell we were or what we were talking about.

All of the pleading in the world wasn't going to change things. We got ripped off.

Defeated, we backed off the porch and down the steps. The door slammed and we heard a cackle inside. She sounded like a witch.

We rounded the garage and saw the streetlight illuminate a perfectly shoveled drive. Then, out of the blue, we mustered an unexpected energy. Justice had to be served. Dinner was calling and we weren't coming. We had more work to do. For some reason, cold and fatigue were gone. We buried that driveway in the snow that we had previously removed and then added more snow from elsewhere. This wasn't your fresh fallen snow, it was packed!

Days later, even the competition couldn't chisel away our concrete-like concoction.

Ski Jogging

One of our favorite winter activities we enjoyed while growing up was what we called "ski jogging."

Once the snow fell, we'd walk the streets, lingering around stop signs when cars would come to a complete stop. Then, at the drop of a dime, a couple of us would break from the pack, ducking and twisting behind the stopped vehicle. In a crouched position, gloved hands clinging to the underside of the back bumper, we'd brace for the ride to begin.

The car, seconds later, would kick snow back at us from under the rear tires as it searched for traction. It was hard not to smile. Often, slush would spray me while my mouth was wide open as I grinned at my ride partner. As the car picked up speed, our boots became skis and we'd glide across the snow packed roads for a block or two. Sometimes we'd wipe out and fly off to the side of the road or up onto a snow-covered lawn. Other times, we'd just let go to reduce the distance to get back to the pack. It was key to have a couple people remain walking so that drivers wouldn't wonder where everyone went ...unless a driver stopped and said for EVERYBODY to get on. This happened from time to time.

One time we all got an offer to ski jog at once. An old car pulled up and the guy rolled his window down and exuberantly offered for us to grab on.

There were six of us. It was difficult to get everybody squeezed in behind the vehicle but we did.

We clutched the bumper and yelled, "Go!"

Well, he must have really wanted to give us a good run because he spun those tires and lurched forward and, apparently, never looked back. Had he looked back, he'd have seen six kids still in a crouched position with his rear bumper in their hands.

The only time we'd ever get injured doing this stunt was when the roads had bare spots. There was nothing worse than cruising in packed or powdery snow and unexpectedly hitting pavement. Fortunately, bare spots were usually just that — spots. It would be just enough to throw off your center of gravity but before you lost your footing, you were past the bare spot and could recover. Otherwise, you'd tumble into a ditch.

When we grew older, there were kids in the neighborhood — older brothers of friends — who had just gotten drivers licenses. Someone concocted the idea of actually skiing from the back of a station wagon. I went for a ride. Kneeling and looking out of the back window, my job was to keep an eye out for other cars, especially cop cars. If I spotted one, I'd give the two skiers a signal, they'd let go and I'd reel in one rope while a friend reeled in the other. The two skiers would coast to a stop, shove the skis under snow and just act like they were chatting with each other.

It worked like a charm except for one time.

When we gave the signal, one guy aborted as planned but, the other was stuck. His sleeve, glove or something was snagged or frozen to the rope. We never quite figured out why he couldn't shake loose. He became frantic, lost his balance when he hit a pile of snow someone had shoveled from their driveway and resembled an old TV skiing clip, aptly named, the "agony of defeat." His body tumbled in a dust of snow and then was dragged, sometimes catching a bit of air as he hit other random piles of snow.

This all transpired in the seconds it took to yell for the driver to stop.

And that was a split second before another yelled, "Cop!"

So the car didn't stop.

The driver panicked and sped up and around a corner he went. The increased momentum turning the corner – car fishtailing – broke the poor skier free but his body was flung into a bunch of bushes lining the front of a house on the corner. He disappeared into them and we disappeared around the block.

When we came back for the rescue, we had to stop, run up to the bushes and fish this poor soul out. He was cut up pretty badly but otherwise okay.

I don't remember ever seeing anyone skiing from the back of a moving vehicle again. Ski jogging, on the other hand …

Streaking

Streaking was a pop culture fad. This involved public nakedness. We had seen it happen spontaneously during professional sporting events or shown in a newspaper or on the evening news, albeit censored. It was a craze to say the least.

On our street we were gathered at a friend's house, bored, on a hot summer day. Nobody had central air conditioning in their houses at this time that I was aware of. We had had our fun with the hose and now just laid in the shade, dripping, wondering what to do next.

"Hey Rocky, I dare you to ride your bike two houses down, naked," challenged a friend.

"If I do, you do three houses," I immediately volleyed back.

There was a pause.

"Deal but we keep going until someone gives," he said, cock sure of himself.

Everyone was on their feet, excited as hell and so the challenge began.

I rode first to the roaring approval of everyone. Mind you it was broad daylight. My friend went next and did three houses but hammed it up on his bike putting both feet on one pedal as he coasted by sticking his ass out at us like he was mooning which was funny because he was stark naked. I tried to out-do his ride. A car passed me beeping like mad. It sounded like approval but I wasn't sure. I couldn't see the people inside.

Eventually, my friend rode half the street and I said he won. He seemed very pleased. Actually, we all were. It was a rollicking good time. In fact, we decided to move the streaking to the football field behind Learwood Junior High School. We ditched our bikes, broke into the concession stand through one of the plywood covered windows. Then we jimmied the trap door loose (we did this all the time) to get to the upper, open levels. On the third deck up, everyone stripped down to their birthday suits. We ran around jumping from floor to floor, exhilarated.

This gave way to naked racing across the football field. That's when someone noticed the door to the field house was cracked open. This was a metal pole barn where all of the track and field equipment was stored. There were mountains of thick pillow-like mats for the high jump and other pads and things. We made a mini indoor obstacle course that started with a naked "Nestea plunge" into the mats, a couple of hurdles, etc. Jacob racked his nuts really bad on the hurdles and was near tears.

We kept going, saying, "shake it off," laughing like crazy.

Our lookout, peeking through the partially open door, sounded a warning.

"Somebody's coming!"

We hid up high – all of us.

The big sliding door was pushed open by a man. He started rummaging for something. Before he even spotted us we panicked in what appeared to be in unison, the chain reaction was so quick!

"Geronimo!"

"Look out below!"

One by one, we plunged to the multi-layered stack of cushions we had created out of big puffy mats. Bouncing and rolling before sprinting out the door – buck naked – we passed this man. He was just plain stunned, paralyzed by shock, I presumed.

We streaked 50 or more yards, downfield, to the field house to retrieve our clothes. That's when Kyle directed us to get over the fence to our bicycles. He scaled the flights of steps to retrieve everyone's stuff. Scaling the fence, naked, was pretty risky business. It wasn't a normal chain-link fence, it was a tall one meant to keep trespassers out.

Clothes rained down but only half fell on our side of the fence.

Once Kyle got down and whipped the clothes and shoes that didn't make it over, over to us, we rapidly dressed, looking around for the man. He was still motionless, but now he stood just outside the pole barn. He was too far to read anything else into it except that we could take our time now and catch our breath. So we did.

That's the only time (or day) we streaked. I can't say the same for shooting the moon!

Pleasure Attic

I was walking home after school. Another classmate, Todd, walked with me. I didn't really know what to make of him. Although he was in my grade, he was nearly two years older than me. I was young for my grade and he, well, was on his second tour of duty.

He asked me if I wanted to come over to his house.

I was a latchkey kid and had nothing better to do so I said, "Sure."

It would be another hour or so before my mom and dad would get home. My sister had a babysitter. I didn't. It saved my parents money.

Todd's mom wasn't home and neither was his older brother.

Although it was nice outside, he invited me in, saying, "Want to see something really cool?"

He grinned, ran upstairs and opened a closet door at the end of the hall. He removed a shelf and popped out a panel (tiny door) in the back of the closet gaining access to a crawl space.

He looked back at me and said, "You can't tell anyone about this."

"I'm not a narc," I said and crawled in after him, curious.

He fumbled around in the dark feeling for something. Then, he held up a hand and flicked a lighter until the sparks turned to flame. He slowly lowered it to light a candle sitting on a saucer.

"Watch yourself so you don't fall through. Stay on the path here and follow me," he directed.

Along the way, he lit more candles leaving a trail of light. We must have backtracked next to the hallway, the length of the bungalow home. The roof was angled over our tight crawl space until we reached a cubbyhole area. It was wider and the slanted ceiling extended higher. There was plenty of room to sit upright. Todd lit a circle of candles.

"This is cool isn't it?" he asked.

I assured him it was. I had never seen anything like it. The secrecy, adventure and mystery all appealed to my thrill-seeking spirit.

"My brother can't know we were here so don't tell anyone. He won't notice if we sneak some of his stash though. Don't tell anyone about this either," Todd said.

I didn't know what he was talking about. I was too busy checking out the nude magazines stacked in in the corners of the lair. I don't know why, but the set-up and placement of the magazines made me think of a waiting room at a doctor's office.

"Beer or pot?"

My eyes bulged and I broke into an instant sweat. Maybe it was because we were in the attic or maybe it was because I was staring at the two choices he had displayed in front of me. I thought this wasn't so cool after all. I wanted out. I wondered how to get out of there without freaking him out.

I certainly wasn't going to do drugs so pot was out of the question.

"Beer," I answered.

He handed me one and popped the top on his. They were warm to the touch but I didn't know enough to know they should be chilled. I don't think he did either. I did know that I couldn't drink beer any more than I could smoke a joint.

"Beer makes me want to pee," I ad-libbed, yet to open the beer he handed me.

He laughed and said, "Aint that the truth."

I told him, "Really, I gotta take a leak."

He looked frustrated with me, "Why didn't you say so earlier?"

I told him I'd be quick and that I knew the way down, no problem. "Be back in a flash."

"I'm drinking yours if you're not," he yelled my way as I crawled around the corner, squinting my eyes when I returned to daylight.

I made a bee line for the door and never looked back.

The Paper Route

As we walked home from school, I saw a lady by a parked car and noticed that she was asking kids questions as they walked by her. When we stopped, she didn't pay any attention to me. She sized up Jacob and asked if he would like to deliver newspapers. Jacob said no.

I waited for her to look at me, but she looked past – rather over – me to the next group nearing. So I spoke up and said I wanted to do it. After confirming I was old enough and running through a list of other questions, she reluctantly gave me the job. Probably, by this time, she noticed no other prospects were headed her way.

She met with my parents later.

Before delivering the afternoon paper, I had to shadow the carriers giving up the route. My territory combined what two brothers used to cover.

Weekday papers were light. I could fit them all in my paper-bag which I wore over one shoulder. Unlike the movies, I had to walk each newspaper to the door of every house. On Sundays, I'd have to stuff parts of the paper together, load a wagon and deliver what was more like a pile of telephone books. Not only that but Sunday subscribers far outnumbered daily subscribers.

Getting my wagon through snowy streets was the worst. Delivering in rain was second worst. That said, there were plenty of other bad – and some not so bad – encounters over time.

Back in those days, the paperboy had to collect. That meant going door-to-door to get your customers to pay up for their subscription. Some went easy and some were delinquent as hell. On my very first round of collecting, a nasty old man dropped every curse word in the book on me when I came to his door. He screamed in my face so long and hard, if I had a nickel for every time he lobbed the "F" word, I could've retired on the spot. I reported the incident to my lady supervisor and he was taken off my route.

Another man stopped his truck next to me on the street to ask to get added back to the route. He must have noticed I was a new carrier. He had a reputation like the old man that was just fired from my route, according to others in the neighborhood. Part of the paperboy's job was to prospect for new subscribers. This guy was nice to me so I added a customer. He was always friendly and paid on time.

A strange family with two boys, one a year older than I and the other two or three years older, were on my route. The reason I call them strange is when I came collecting one day, their parents invited me inside. They all gathered around and treated me kindly as if I were company they were expecting. They even treated me to Rocky Road candy. The mom made it sound like she made it special for me since my name was Rocky. I didn't want to be rude so I ate it and they watched. None of them had any. I felt very uncomfortable. As I sat on the couch, it seemed they didn't want me to leave. I entertained the possibility that I might have been poisoned so they could abduct me or do something to me. So, I eyed up the window. I would lunge my body through it if they closed in on me. Later, I laughed it off as me being paranoid.

The next day, the oldest boy walked down the driveway as I walked up with the newspaper. He smiled and slammed a fist smack in the middle of my face. I stood, stunned, as he ordered me to never step one foot in his yard again.

Then there were the really kind people – sometimes, too kind. One was a high school girl, very pretty. She invited me in, kissed me long and hard and then smiled and disappeared into the back of the house. I stood, silent and awestruck for the longest time. She didn't return so I left.

Another joyous occasion was when a fairly attractive single woman answered the door in a towel when I was collecting. The towel dropped as she fetched her purse and I got an eyeful. She didn't look one bit embarrassed and merely said, "Oops," rewrapped herself and paid me, smiling. I was smiling, too.

When I had a doctor's appointment, my mom would type up a note that we stapled to the front of every paper the day before explaining why the newspaper would be an hour late the next day. The two former paper boys thought I was showing them up, I guess, because they threatened to kick my butt if I did it again. I did it again but they didn't seem to notice.

The scariest encounter I ever had was while I delivered the paper to a trucker's house. I came to the porch to put the paper between the doors and he flung it open in my face as if he had been waiting all afternoon for me to show up. He was livid to say the least, convinced that I had stolen thousands of dollars' worth of tools from his garage. I really thought he might kill me right there in broad daylight. He was not going to let me go until I admitted my crime. But I had no crime to admit. He said the only person who could possibly know what was in his garage was the paperboy. I think it was because the paperboy would be the only possible person to get close enough to the garage to get a peek inside. I wondered about the two brothers who had the route before me. Somehow, after a long interrogation, he must have wondered, too.

My biggest mistake while having this paper route was not remembering a customer telling me that he was going on vacation and needed the paper stopped while he was gone. I simply forgot by the time I finished my route that day. After stuffing nearly a week of newspapers between his front storm and screen doors, I planned to call my supervisor to see what I should do if the papers kept piling up. It was to the point that I had to be super quick – open the screen door, flip a paper inside and shut it before all of them poured out. As I approached the house, I noticed a car in the driveway. I was relieved. When I walked up, I was met by a very unhappy customer. He said for me to come back with my mom or dad. When we returned, he held a contained anger while he lectured me on how the papers piling up had advertised nobody was home and that his house could have been robbed. In the end, he forgave me.

All and all, the paper route was a great experience in so many ways. I made a habit of reading the front page stories on a daily basis while walking my route. One day, some kids had news before me.

They ran by yelling, "The President was shot – the President was shot ..."

It Better Be Broken!

Fall meant football and we played the game with gusto; no helmets, no pads, full contact! Sometimes, we'd send someone home early – or worse.

It was easy to gather a bunch of kids in our neighborhood to play a game at the school lot. Green grass turned to brown soup before long. There was pride in coming home covered in mud from head to toe and told to strip to your shorts before entering the house.

Many injuries happened throughout those years. Heck, someone got hurt every game or so it seemed. About once a year, someone got to sport a cast as a result of a lick they took.

One day, an older kid and his buddies decided to play with us. They were two, maybe three years our senior. It didn't matter because that's just what happened in our neighborhood. Besides, we had mixed teams. It wasn't like it was us against them. But one guy was a bulldozer. Nobody could bring him down unless it was a gang tackle. I decided that would stop.

I flew out into the flat to greet him on a screen pass. As soon as he caught the ball our bodies slammed together. You could feel bone on bone. I wrapped him up and refused to let go. It slowed him enough for reinforcements to arrive. The pile moved and then tipped. Somewhere in the entanglement of bodies, my arm twisted and we all heard the familiar sound of a "branch" snapping in two.

We peeled off the pack one by one to pan the crowd for the face that rang out pain. All eyes were on me.

"Rock, you better get that checked out."

"Na, it'll be all right," I said.

My skin wasn't ruptured, no bone was showing, my arm seemed straight. I figured it was a sprain and I could shake it off.

Two plays later, I was on my bike, riding left-handed, cradling my right arm. Every crack in the sidewalk shot sharp pain straight to my forearm. The ride was sheer agony. What made it worse was knowing that the pain was coming over and over, but I had no choice but to keep riding. The street was too busy so I had to stay the course on the sidewalk.

This was Saturday afternoon. Dad worked most Saturday mornings and sometimes took a nap when he got home. My timing was perfect. Dad's door was closed but the pain was enough to roust him.

A groggy voice spoke through the closed door, "You'll be all right. Wait 'til your mother gets home."

I sat on the couch and waited for what seemed like an eternity.

Mom came home but was in the middle of a list of things that HAD to get done.

"What? Broken. I don't think so," she was in denial.

She wasn't convinced it was broken but we were headed to the hospital anyway. On the way, she muttered under her breath. I could tell she was upset with the turn in her day. She really thought I had only sprained my arm so going to the hospital was a waste of time.

Finally, she looked over at me, frustrated, and deadpanned, "It better be broken."

As we waited for results, I kept repeating in my head, "Please be broken, please be broken, please be broken."

It was! Clean through. And another bone had a large chip in it.

Whew!

Caddy Days

I was called into the principal's office at my middle school to be told that I was too young to work, according to child labor laws. So, I had to quit my job as a caddy at a nearby country club. Instead, I rode my bike twice the distance to caddy at a different country club across the county line – at least until school let out for summer vacation. Then, I returned to the closer place, which was still a long bike ride.

As I left Avon Lake on a country road, over the railroad tracks, I pedaled as fast as I could down the slope on the other side. I had to gain enough speed to coast by an old farmhouse with my feet up by my handlebars. There he was, barking and running right into the road, nipping at my empty pedals. No sooner than he gave up the chase did my momentum slow enough to force my feet back to the pedals. It was always a close call.

At the caddy shack, the caddy master called me over to a foursome ready for a loop. There was snickering behind the first tee. Later, I heard that someone had intentionally matched a preacher with a foul-mouth. Not until the third hole did the foul-mouth know he was in the company of a man of the cloth. That's when everyone except the foul-mouth burst into laughter. Soon, more cursing drowned out the laughter. Later, I heard people say they could even hear the laughter and cursing all the way back at the clubhouse.

My golfer was on the quiet side compared to the others. I didn't know if he was new, subordinate or just quiet by nature. He was a stroke or two in last. I handed him a wedge for a chip shot out of the sand trap. He got a hold of that thing and it screamed out of there so fast and hard that I thought I might have to yell, "Fore!"

It ricocheted off an oak branch overhead abruptly sending it into the flag of the pin where it fell straight down into the cup. It happened in the blink of an eye. I had never seen anything like it so I broke character and roared in delight. It was a fantastic shot in my mind. When I caught the facial expression of my golfer, I was puzzled because he looked downright embarrassed.

I asked him, off to the side, "Wasn't that incredible?"

He gave me half a smile on the sly, tasseled my hair and walked to the next tee. Later, he tipped me the most I ever got that summer.

After my morning round, I decided to hang out for some caddy baseball and try to get a second loop after lunch. One of the caddies in this group was just plain tough as nails. He was older than I and from the inner city. His golfer was one of those who had to insult people to act like a big shot, and he demeaned his caddies.

Nobody wanted to caddy for him but inner city caddy said, "I don't give a shit, a loop's a loop."

It was a scorcher of an afternoon so we rolled up our short sleeves to try and fade out the infamous caddy-tan lines on our arms. Inner city caddy was sporting homemade tattoos.

His golfer insisted he keep his sleeves down, "A little more class here, boy."

I saw inner city caddy drop a mouthful of spit into the guy's golf bag when nobody else was looking. He took a lot more abuse than I figured he could stand. I began to think he must really need to make a buck. He sucked it up, rebelled a little behind the scenes and marched on like a real trooper.

It was somewhere along the back nine that fate and justice crossed paths.

The big-shot golfer sliced a shot off the fairway into a tree. You could see the ball fall down but not out. It rested on a branch about 15-feet-high. The golfer out cursed the morning foul-mouth. During his tirade, he spun around and released his iron. The golf club flung round and round, landing in a pond.

"Get my club! Then, get my ball!" he said to the inner city kid.

To his credit, the kid casually walked to the pond, never uttering a word. Then, he turned and waited for the golfer to look.

"Come on, come on, we don't have all day," the golfer said for the kid to hear.

That wasn't all that he said. When he turned toward his friends, under his breath, he added something about that kind being lazy. His friends didn't look at him. They looked past him and nodded that he better look for himself, too.

The kid was standing with the entire golf bag, and all of its very expensive contents, over his head.

"What the …"

Before the big shot could finish his sentence, the kid spun around much like the golfer did before he launched his club. Only this time, it was the kid launching the entire bag …deep into the pond. Then, he turned, flashed two flagrant middle fingers and walked off into the sun, never to be seen again.

The Lady in the Bathtub

My parents moved in and shortly thereafter one of their next door neighbors told my dad a disturbing story about my parents' house – a lady died in the bathtub. According to this neighbor's story, the lady's husband called him over as soon as he found her dead. This neighbor went on to tell of some suspicious circumstances later recounted by another neighbor.

About this same time, one of the young daughters from the other next door neighbor joined my mom on the front steps and said, "A lady drowned in your bathtub."

Later in the day, the girl's mother found out about her daughter's loose lips, got upset, apologized and then filled in the details.

The stories basically told to my parents were that this lady was widely assumed to have had a drinking problem. On the day in question, she was apparently taking a bath. Her husband was in the next room. After her death, the body was soon cremated and he remarried just a few months later. So, it makes for a suspicious story. Was she drunk and someone held her under? A whiskey bottle was supposedly next to the tub. One neighbor called it straight up murder.

Whether any of the details are true, we don't know for sure but what we do know for sure is that a lady died in the bathtub we used. Suffice it to say, this grisly fact was not disclosed by the Realtor.

At the time, our house had only one full bathroom so we HAD to take showers in the "death tub." Needless to say, my sister and I skipped a few cleanings. And when we did have to shower, we'd have the other stand in the hallway, outside the closed door listening for any yells for help. I used to burn my eyes regularly when they should have been closed more tightly while shampooing. I'd feel a hand on my head pushing me under the water and realize it was my own. I used to shower in less than two minutes flat for at least a year after being told this horrific story.

Of course, we shared the story with friends who would sleep-over. All of them would nearly tumble, rushing out of the bathroom after they had to use it, looking over their shoulder to see if "The Lady in the Bathtub" was following.

I was a few years older than my sister. One of her friends suggested they play a little game called "Bloody Mary." They dared me and I accepted. How could I not?

Our bathroom was so dark when you pulled the door closed and turned off the lights, it was black as black could be. You truly couldn't see your hand in front of your face. It wasn't a large bathroom. You could walk in and the towel rack, sink and toilet were to the left and the bath tub to the right. When you looked into the mirror, the bathtub reflected in it.

I stood facing the mirror in the pitch black chanting for the girls outside to hear. I had to say "Bloody Mary" 50 times out loud, staring into the mirror. I couldn't even see my own face it was so dark. At some point, I was supposed to come face-to-face with "Bloody Mary," but there was a whole different level of terror running through my veins. I expected to see the reflection of "The Lady in the Bathtub" appear from over my shoulder, reaching out from the bathtub to grab me and pull me in to sure death by drowning. I said "Bloody Mary" for the 17th time and rushed out to safety unable to be in that room a split second longer.

Everyone laughed but it's a record that was never broken!

If Looks Could Kill

If the four of us didn't affirm what just happened, I wouldn't have believed my own eyes and ears.

We were traveling cross country in the family van. Up early to put some pavement between us and our last stop, we grew hungry – really hungry – so Dad decided we would find a restaurant to enjoy a nice breakfast. It was Sunday around the time church let out and people flocked to town eateries.

We parked. I had a skip in my step, excited at the thought of the whopping stack of pancakes I was going to order. We passed the front windows of the restaurant. It was full of people. We could hear the chattering of voices and clanking of silverware.

A young lady met us at the door and immediately led us to a table, not a booth, in the middle of the restaurant. As we walked to our table, the place grew quieter and quieter. We sat and were told the waitress would be with us in a moment.

It was a long moment.

In that time, the four of us grew quiet as well. It felt like people were staring at us. I looked around. They were. If a fork fell to a plate now, the noise would pierce the deafening silence. My eyes searched for comfort and protection. They locked on Mom and Dads' as did my sister's. They had a blank gaze.

The waitress still didn't come. The full restaurant still didn't make a sound. Nobody so much as ate. They just watched us in silence. My heart raced. My skin crawled.

"Leave – Now," Dad said under his breath but we all heard it loud and clear.

Dad got up and so did we. All of our heads were down as we whisked out the door.

When we hit the sidewalk along the front windows, the inside of the restaurant sounded as it had on approach. Voices chattered in conversation, dishes clanked and all was normal.

"What the heck just happened?"

None of us could reason an answer.

We laughed about it, uncomfortably.

Dad drove like a bat out of hell (town).

I didn't mind my hunger pains.

CHAPTER 2:
WILD TIMES IN HIGH SCHOOL

Prank Calls

There was a time when we only had one phone per household and when it rang, you had to answer because you would otherwise have no idea who was calling.

My first encounter with a prank (rather, obscene) caller was when I was playing at my friend Jacob's house. His mom asked him to answer the phone as she scooted by with an arm full of laundry. We were only in grade school at the time. The caller asked Jacob a series of questions that progressively got more personal. When Jacob's mom walked back in the room she reached for the phone asking Jacob who it was.

"I don't know but he asked what color panties you had," Jacob answered.

My eyes bugged out.

Jacob's mom was a saintly woman but she increased my vocabulary in just the brief statement she shouted into the phone before slamming it down.

Years later, although we were never seedy or obscene, we, like many kids, made prank calls. I actually used to call them crank calls. There are two that stuck with me. One happened in junior high school and the other happened in high school.

The most elaborate prank we learned was the ole, "We have workers on the telephone lines nearby."

It went like this: "We're just calling to let you know that we have workers on the telephone lines nearby. Please stay off the phone and definitely don't answer if it rings in the next five minutes."

Almost always, the trusting party on the other end would say okay, albeit some were somewhat perplexed.

We'd wait almost the entire five minutes and call back. If the phone rang and rang – answering machines were rare back then – we'd be disappointed that they heeded our warning. If the same person picked up the phone, we were ready. We'd waive a hair dryer back and forth and then scream like hell and kill the line by hanging up.

A minute later we'd call again. If they didn't answer this time, we'd laugh our devious heads off. If they did answer, we usually couldn't get in a word edgewise as they apologized profusely. At least we left them reassured that everything was fine.

In high school, radio station phone contest giveaways were common. You could be the recipient of a random outbound call or be caller number 100 for example, if the station was 100 FM. A few of us were listening to music one night in a friend's bedroom. We decided to prank some people and then came up with an idea to pretend we were radio disc jockeys.

Our first call was to a young-sounding woman, maybe in high school.

I forget the hot concert tour of the time but we told her, "CONGRATULATIONS, this is *so and so* at FM (name of a station) and you are our random call."

She pierced our ears with excitement, "AGHHH – what I win, what I win …?"

"Brace yourself because you and a friend are going to see …!"

Her reaction nearly made us go deaf listening together on our end. She had to put someone else on the line – while she hyperventilated – so we could confirm details to send the tickets but we didn't write a thing down on our end.

When this sensational phone prank ended, we were beside ourselves in how well it went. Then, our conscience took hold and nearly five minutes later, we felt so bad we decided we had to suck it up, call back and let this poor soul off the hook.

But we didn't remember her phone number.

Big Shots

It's funny, but I don't remember any of my childhood friends or classmates being Cleveland Indians baseball fans. Maybe it was too painful to admit openly.

When I was in high school, the manager was probably best remembered for charging the mound at an opposing pitcher, pathetically failing to land a karate kick. To add insult to injury, the pitcher dropped our manager with one punch. But this was my team, my lovable losers. I played in a world of possibility whereas nearly everyone else I knew played in a world of probability. Life is safer their way. But perhaps it's with my mindset that I entered an essay contest by a Cleveland newspaper – "Why Do You Like The Indians?" At this age, I was reading the sports section daily so I wrote and sent in my essay.

I won!

Thinking back, I wonder if I was the only one who bothered with the contest.

Nonetheless, the prize was "dinner" with the Indians and a free ballgame. Dinner with the Indians meant I got to invite a friend to accompany me to the stadium for a luncheon that launched the team's winter press tour. Only the manager and a couple players showed up to talk to the room full of reporters and afterward, I got to wait in line to shake the hand of a forgettable rookie infielder.

When we got there, Mom dropped us off and my friend, Steve, and I walked in. Immediately, we seized a plush booth. It was long – very long – and center stage. It was located in the back of the room next to huge windows high above the ground outside. It had our names all over it, so to speak. It was ours! Until some lackey in a suit scrambled across the room to us as some old guy and his entourage entered.

"Hey kids, you can't sit there!" he said with alarm.

"Sure we can," I said.

"We are," said Steve, shooting a smile my way knowing he just slipped in a cocky remark under the radar.

The man demanded we move.

"But I won the contest," I said matter of fact.

He looked dumbfounded. Then, he saw the entourage nearing and looked back to us in desperation.

"You gotta go, now," he pleaded, reaching for my arm.

I pulled away and scooted farther into the wrap-around booth.

"What seems to be the problem?" asked the old man arriving next to the table. His entourage fanned out around it.

The scared looking man (lackey) sounded like he had diarrhea of the mouth so I explained.

Laughing, the old man said, "You boys have a good time," and he left us to the enormous booth.

Then, he and his entourage pulled tables and chairs together in the center of the room, displacing some adults.

As they crowded around a hastily made large table by clustering together smaller tables right in front of us, we sat back and ordered meals fit for kings. I sat at one end of the long booth and Steve sat on the far end. You could have sat five adults on one side between us.

This was our day and nobody was going to take it away.

Later, the old man was introduced as the general manager of the Cleveland Indians. My natural instinct was to boo, but I bit my tongue. We all knew how the Indians were mishandled, but I couldn't help but appreciate the kindness he extended toward us.

On the way out, Steve and I shared an elevator with a "rising star." He had a giggling girl under each arm, thereby making him a bigger hero than just a moment earlier, even though he didn't notice us in the tight space we shared going down.

Sunset Park

She said she'd be back as soon as she could sneak out.

I kicked back on my sleeping bag as the streetlights came on, listening to Pink Floyd's *Comfortably Numb* through my headphones. About an hour later, it was dark and I was enjoying the peace of the night, alone.

Every now and then, I'd see headlights running parallel to the front of the park. I was as far back as you could go, nestled under some trees and against a natural barrier separating the park from the houses in the subdivision behind it. More time passed. I was getting sleepy and barely paid attention to another passing car – until it stopped.

My attention came into focus even though I was sure nobody could see me in the dark, not from the front of the park anyway. The headlights reversed and under a streetlight I saw that it was a police car. I perked up and slowly slid my legs free from the sleeping bag. The car reversed into a side street pointing its headlights to the back of the park. I couldn't believe it. Immediately, I lay low and still. The lights grew brighter. The car was driving through the grass directly at me.

I got up and ran.

When I got to the edge of the park, I cut the corner and ran to a friend's house that bordered the park. He slept in a basement bedroom so I knocked on his window. He didn't answer. He may not have been home now that I thought about it.

The police car sailed quickly by my position down a sidewalk that led from the park to the subdivision behind it, right next to my friend's house.

I ran again.

The police car hit the street and whipped around the corner, no doubt catching a glimpse of me on the other side darting behind a line of houses. I ran through the backyards all the way to the end and then circled back a couple of houses and peaked around. The police car was circling back too. He knew he had me pinned down somewhere back there. His car went back and forth in shorter distances as if somehow he was narrowing his search. When he drove back up the road, I bolted across it. I saw the headlights spin around and come in my direction again. I hid in a tunnel under a connecting road until he passed again. This time, he made the zigzag and followed the road further down. That's when I sprinted to the woods and headed north again in the direction of the park but west of it. My adrenaline was pumping and so were my feet and heart. I blazed a trail in the dark and paid for it. My arms and face were stinging from the branches whipping me as I made my way to who knows where.

Finally, I stumbled on a trail and I knew where it led.

Once I escaped the woods, I went to the house of the girl who was supposed to meet me in the park. In her backyard there was a step ladder leaned against the house just under her window. It was only a one-story house. I laughed. This was how she was going to sneak out. I stepped up the ladder and whispered through the open window into her room. She was sound asleep so I whispered louder and louder.

Finally, she lifted her head, startled. Then her eyes settled on my silhouette. She invited me inside. We figured it was too risky to sleep out as planned. So, I crashed there for the rest of the night. In the morning, I had to hide in a closet from her mom.

After her mom left for work, we went to the park to retrieve my things but they were gone.

Somehow, I felt lucky.

Three Choices

I was given three choices. He would vandalize my parents' house, kick the shit out of me or kill me.

We were in high school and I had fallen in with a troubled kid in the neighborhood. After school one day, I showed him my dad's amazing, award-winning, tropical fish in what we called the fish room but was really most of the basement. There was a razor blade on a worktable and this dude picked it up and started swiping it in the air like a maniac, uttering who knows what. He actually sliced through something of my dad's. I yelled for him to stop. Instead, he turned and swiped downward, slicing open the sleeve of my new winter jacket. The slash was long. My jacket was ruined. I was angry.

He dropped the razor blade and ran upstairs, laughing a demented laugh the whole while. I picked up the blade, gave chase and tackled him on the living room couch. That's when I swiped downward to cut his jacket sleeve as he had done mine. Call it revenge.

I accidentally ripped through more than just his jacket. The razor also sliced through his flannel shirt, sinking into the top of his forearm. Thank goodness his arm wasn't twisted another way. Still, the blood was frightening to us both. More frightening was how the thick layers of skin, and probably muscle, spread open. I apologized profusely as I applied whatever I could find from our medicine cabinet. He later got medical attention but the resulting scar was long, wide and red.

After that, I was a marked man.

He threatened me constantly. Often he cited the three choices he was offering: Vandalize my parents' house, kick the shit out of me or kill me.

One spring night he tore out all of my parents flowers up front so the taunt was altered to, "Vandalize my parents' house AGAIN!"

He was much bigger than I and seemed pretty unstable. I did not want to take any of the choices he offered but our paths crossed too often to avoid him. We had classes together. I went to my parents for help. Dad told me that unfortunately, I would probably have to have it out with him.

His pep talk involved things about what's in my blood, my roots, the bigger they come the harder they fall, and finished with, "Don't tangle at school, though, if you can help it."

Well, I sure didn't sleep that night. I knew I could fight. I had done plenty of it to defend myself in the past. I only started one fight in my life and lost. Dad had no sympathy for that. He said I got what I deserved. Never start a fight — but always finish. The next day was finishing day.

After a science test, we had free time to just socialize about the classroom before the "tone" went off to change classes. I was with my friend, Steve, near one corner in the back of the room.

My nemesis calmly and confidently walked between us, sat on one of the long black lab tables stretching across the entire back of the room and said, "So Satullo, did you decide? What's it going to be …" and he rattled off the three choices I had.

As my nemesis remained sitting on the table, he looked at me and repeated my choices. So, I made my choice with an uppercut to his chin. He rolled backward over the table and I leaped it, following punch after punch into the side of his head. Every blow knocked him back and I followed, all the way across the back of the room until a massive body flung me to the side and my nemesis ran from the room. The teacher who separated us wielded around and gave me a look that could kill. The air was thick with testosterone as we locked eyes.

The moment was interrupted by several students who had followed my nemesis to the bathroom, "I think you broke his jaw." …"I think you broke his nose." …"You're in deep shit, Satullo."

All of us still in the classroom were directed by the teacher to get cleaning supplies and as a class, we scrubbed the back wall which looked like a B-movie blood bath with spray patterns marking every blow I delivered.

Later, my nemesis and I sat in the vice-principal's office. The vice-principal kept silent as he read the report given to him. Occasionally, he'd look up and then look down again to be sure he knew who was who.

"Let me get this straight, YOU beat up HIM?"

We were made to call our parents to get picked up from school immediately to begin our suspensions. I was standing next to the vice-principal at his desk when he handed me the phone to talk to my mom.

"Are you okay?" she asked.

"Yes."

"Did you win?"

I was too embarrassed to answer.

She kept repeating the question. Her voice could be heard across the room through the phone receiver.

Eventually I whispered, "Yes."

Happiness and relief erupted through the phone receiver.

I handed the phone back to the vice-principal and sank low into a chair.

Rumors circulated going into summer that it wasn't over. Supposedly, my nemesis had something to carry out choice number three if our paths crossed.

I'm Not Drunk!

A few doors down, an older high school friend invited me over along with others. I knew there would be beer there.

The friend stepped out and came back in the side door with two cases over his head. His smile was as wide as the room. Everyone roared. One case slipped and crashed to the floor. So it was set just outside the sliding doors as we gathered around a table with a glass and quarter for a drinking game.

It was the first time I ever drank alcohol. After a while, I thought I must have some sort of superman endurance because I felt no effect, but I did have to pee.

In the bathroom, I stared at myself in the mirror, somewhat judgmental, somewhat as hypnotist and said out loud to my reflection, "You are not drunk. You are not drunk. You are not drunk."

When I returned, I felt like I was walking on the deck of a ship at sea. Like a sailor, I continued to toss back beer like it was the last night of leave. I also made return trips to the bathroom to pee. Eventually, even I knew I was kidding the man in the mirror.

Walking home, my arms seemed to go up and down at supersonic speed with every step. A car drove by. Although the speed limit was only 25 MPH, I only saw trailing lights.

It was Saturday night so my parents were still up watching a movie in the family room when I entered through the kitchen.

"I'm going straight to bed. Goodnight," I called to them.

Once upstairs, I hit my bed. The spinning was unbearable. I turned and it got worse. I closed my eyes and felt acid make it to the top of my throat but I kept it down. Like a geyser, eventually the pressure had nowhere to go but up. I painted the wall, bed, floor and everything within a seven foot radius.

Mom and Dad stood in the doorway.

"H-E-L-P …MEEEEEEE," I pleaded, reaching out to them.

"Are you drunk?" Mom asked, flabbergasted.

"YOU'RE SLEEPING IN IT!" My dad slammed the door on me.

The next thing I remember was waking up to a putrid smell. When I bent over the edge of my bed to dry-heave, I noticed the swamp that used to be shag carpeting. I scanned my room and couldn't wrap my mind around the amount of disgusting muck everywhere, on everything.

I wallowed in my own filth, wondering where the jack-hammer was, and prayed to God I would NEVER drink again.

CHiPs

Once upon a time in TV land, there was a show called, CHiPs. The lead characters, Ponch and John, were motorcycle cops for the California Highway Patrol.

Coming back from downtown Cleveland, my friends wanted me to bring the roof down. They knew that if I got my car to go fast enough, air would balloon the interior ceiling fabric.

I complied.

We were sailing down the highway, whooping and hollering as the bubble began to form.

"Faster-faster!"

A couple of newbies cried out in delight, "Holy ^$%#@ – it's really working!"

Traffic was light so we kept speeding. The ceiling didn't just bubble downward it smashed our heads lower and lower. Laughing hysterically, I was forced so low I was peering between the dashboard and the top of the steering wheel just to see the road ahead. That is until I caught a glimpse of something in my peripheral vision – a motorcycle cop!

Now imagine his perspective. I have no idea what we looked like from the rear of the vehicle upon his approach. But I can imagine how bizarre the sight was when he pulled side-by-side and saw me. That's because as I looked at him, I had about six inches of visibility out that side window. And I probably looked insane from the expression on my face. Of course, that was a split second before my jaw dropped from seeing a motorcycle cop next to me.

Once I pulled over, I wasn't sure of the protocol. I figured it would be courteous to get out and meet the officer so he didn't have to walk so far. It was the first I can remember seeing a motorcycle cop on the highway, or anywhere, other than TV.

I blurted out, "Hey Ponch, where's John?"

He smiled, looked down, shook his head and wrote me a ticket.

The Polish Police Car

As soon as I cleared the intersection, flashing lights appeared in my rear-view mirror. I pulled over knowing I didn't beat the yellow traffic signal.

I was more afraid of answering to my parents than the police. My window was down when the officer appeared out of the darkness. He was laughing so hard, he couldn't form words.

Maybe I'd catch a lucky break, a warning rather than a ticket.

My car was no hot rod, far from it. My parents wouldn't let me drive their vehicles and they wouldn't buy a car for me. I had to earn and save money to come up with the $500 to buy a rusted out clunker. It was powder blue so the rust really stood out. That was until my friends and I taped it up and painted it with 10 cans of spray paint thanks to a loan my little sister floated me from her babysitting money. We bought seven cans of red and three cans of white – just enough to put a racing stripe across the top and hood.

What really set my bucket of bolts apart from any other hell on wheels was its door handles, or lack thereof. Soon after buying my clunker, all four door handles ripped right off the sides of the car due to the rust. I used to shift the remaining innards to open the doors – until my dad gave me sheet metal and a rivet gun. So there you have it, a car with no door handles. We had to get in through the windows.

The officer finally forced out a sentence although gasping for breath, he was laughing so hard.

Bracing himself with one hand clutching my roof, he asked, "Whatta we have here, a polish police car?"

His eyes were watering when he doubled over, holding his gut, laughing heartily.

And I still got a ticket.

Gas Crisis

My tank was on empty, as usual.

Dad gave me 20 bucks to fill 'er up and have a good time. Half of the money was for raking leaves and cutting grass and the other half was just because. It was enough to fill my tank and get into a teenage club open Monday nights.

I pulled into Sohio instead of Gas Town because they advertised a penny less per gallon. The pump was stuck. It read $15. No matter what I did, it would not reset to zero so I couldn't pump my gas. Frustrated, I asked one of my buddies to tell the gas attendant inside to reset the pump so I could gas up.

My buddy came out to relay, "Not until you pay $15."

This made no sense at all. Why would I fill up my car and ask for the meter to be reset so I could fill it up again? But the gas attendant insisted.

So we left.

The next day after school let out, I walked to my car with friends and the juvenile police officer was waiting for me. All the teens in town knew him by name. I had never seen him before. He said I stole gas and now I had to answer for it. I tried to explain but he said I'd have to come to the station later, with a parent, to make my statement. If I didn't, he would come and get me.

When my dad got home from work, I told him the whole story. We were sitting at our dining room table.

He looked me square in the eyes and asked, "Did you steal the gas?"

I insisted that I did not.

"Rocky, I did a lot of things when I was your age so right now I just want the truth. I need to know if you did it or not. You have to level with me."

I looked him square in the eyes and said, "I did not do it."

Dad paused, never taking his eyes off mine, and then said, "I believe you. Now let's go."

Just like that, with nothing but my word, he had my back. I felt like a million bucks.

We were buzzed into the police station. The juvenile cop wasn't there so the person at the reception desk said they'd get another officer. When we were left alone for a moment to wait, my dad smiled at me and said don't worry, I think he's Italian. We both laughed out loud at his joke. Maybe it was a half-joke.

Inside a room, we sat across from Officer "X." From the get-go, "X" was hostile and interrogated me like I was a, a, a thief. I got defensive because I was totally innocent. A hand lightly but firmly squeezed my shoulder. I sat back to look at my dad. He calmly gave me a very slight left-right shake of his head as if to say, that's enough son. I've got it from here.

Then, he let that police officer know what time it was. The whole while he was cool – assertive but cool – and laid it all out plain as day.

Officer "X" shouted at Dad.

Dad got up, pulled my arm to rise with him, and calmly said, "We're done here."

As we started for the door, Officer "X" was taken aback. He stuttered and then spit out for us to stop so we did and turned to face him.

"The owner of the station is going to go through the records at the end of the week and if they are off by $15, we'll be seeing each other again," Officer "X" said.

We never got a call. And to be honest, I never sweated it because Dad had my back.

Cleaning the Place Out

I had a summer job sweeping a shop floor on weeknights in a neighboring town. It was an old building next to the new one where they made enormous bearings. My mom worked days in the office of the new building.

On this night I had my friend Tommy with me because we had a party to go to afterward. He opted to chill in the car while I worked inside. I had been instructed to always pull off the road to the old back entrance to the shop to get inside.

Usually there was one man who worked nights in the old shop, welding or something, but he wasn't there. I flipped the lights on, found a push broom and swept up a sweat.

A while later, broom in motion, a voice from behind made me jump clean out of my skin.

"FREEZE!"

Well, my skin froze.

Gun drawn, the small town cop circled to where I could see him.

"What the hell you doing, kid?"

"Sweeping, sir."

"Bullshit!"

"I work here, sir."

"We'll see about that," he said. "Get your boss on the phone."

It was nighttime. I didn't know anyone's phone number so I called my mom. Mom talked to the policeman but he was still suspicious and said if someone didn't clear me, I'd be in jail until someone could.

Although I was uneasy about this policeman eager for action, I had to remind myself not to laugh out loud at the absurdity of it all. What burglar stops to sweep a floor?

The folly continued much longer than I thought possible but a messenger finally came from the new building next door and relayed from my mom to this messenger's boss that I was cleared. Then, the messenger left to go back to work next door and I stood alone in the empty shop with the policeman again.

"Next time, don't be so suspicious and ..." He went on to lecture me. Lecture! Me!

Finally, he left.

I finished sweeping the shop and went out to my car where Tommy was still handcuffed to the steering wheel.

Springsteen Tickets

It was late at night when we opened our house after a long family vacation.

My best friend, Mike, and I had plans to meet in the morning to go downtown and buy tickets to a Springsteen concert. It would be the first day for tickets to go on sale. This was back when Bruce Springsteen was selling out stadiums in just hours.

A local television news station reported a line already forming around Cleveland Municipal Stadium with people ready to buy tickets the next morning.

It was the middle of the night and I was wide awake. I couldn't wait. So I grabbed my car keys and before I knew it, I was on my way to get Mike – but he didn't know it.

I didn't want to wake up his parents so I climbed on top of their motor home to get on the roof of their house. Mike slept on the second floor. His window overlooked the garage roof so I navigated my way there.

He didn't share his room with anyone but he slept on the top bunk of a bunk bed. His head was right by the open window. The only thing between us was a screen. His dog, Bandit, started to growl – low and then louder. I tried to calm the dog letting him know that he knew this cat burglar. I was afraid he'd wake the whole house if his growling turned into full-fledged barking.

It was dark inside so I didn't see Mike rolling to see what his dog was snarling at. When his eyes met mine only inches away, well, talk about a wake-up call. Imagine opening your eyes from a dead sleep to see a face peering in your window inches from yours. Mike sprang from the mattress, slammed his head on the ceiling and fell off the upper bunk onto the floor.

I almost rolled off the roof in terror myself. Then, I just tried to contain my laughter, which came in snorts as I tried to hold it in. Mike gathered his senses, climbed back to the window and gave me an obscenity-laced greeting, albeit in a whisper-yell.

It was a small miracle that nobody else in the house woke up.

Down at the stadium, we circled the parking lot and found the end of the line where others were camping out. We parked nearby and joined the growing throng of people. Some were better prepared than we were. Leaning up against the concrete wall, sitting on asphalt, soon we realized it would be a long night.

"Ya know, your kind of car, the backseat 'ell pop right out," Mike surmised.

Within minutes we were sitting in hillbilly comfort. Then a guy returned to his group behind us with so many doughnuts, they shared with us. They were the best doughnuts I ever had in my life.

Hours later – most people around us sleeping – I opened my eyes and noticed it was dawn. I got up and stretched. When I did, I drifted out from the building and peered around the corner – nobody was in front of us. I casually walked up to Mike, kicked his foot several times and motioned for him to quietly check it out.

Without words being spoken, we both walked. Our pace quickened. We thought we were sly but our movement didn't go unnoticed. There was a chain reaction. We peeked over our shoulders. A mob was thickening and gaining. We flat out sprinted from there. It probably looked like we were rock stars trying to outrun hundreds of rabid fans, when in reality they just wanted tickets as badly as we did. We turned another corner of the stadium and plunged into a sea of people. Police were holding everyone back.

"If you're on this side of the barricade, I'm sorry, you're not getting tickets," said one cop after another into megaphones. "Please turn around and go home."

People were disgruntled but reluctantly complying, for the most part. Some tested the officers and were met with more forceful directives. We quickly assessed the scene and bolted over a concrete barricade into some sort of cement trench. We were able to run, hunched over, avoiding being seen. I don't know how we found this and why nobody else did but once we were past the police barrier, we sprang from our trench and joined the mob on the other side.

There was only one gate, one turnstile, one ticket window, and thousands of people fighting to get to it.

The head of the production company pleaded over loud speakers, "We don't want another Cincinnati."

He was referring to a concert years ago where people stampeded each other to death.

"If this doesn't get orderly RIGHT NOW, we'll close her down and NOBODY will get tickets," the man was shrieking at the top of his lungs.

The unruly crowd somehow demonstrated just enough civility for the mayhem to continue.

More than an hour later, Mike and I were in the final stretch. We were jammed in like sardines, between two metal railings leading up to the ticket window.

"Give me your money so we can make sure we get tickets together," Mike said.

I didn't want to abandon him but I had an idea. The other side of the railing was relatively calm, believe it or not. I slipped through and then turned to help Mike. The space between the railings was wide enough for one and half bodies. However, there were three and a half in that space, at times with nothing but Mike's ass on the inside. He was getting crushed. Whenever that happened, he fought with flailing elbows and fists, cursing, to regain space so he could breathe. I helped by pushing and shoving people so they'd give him room. It didn't matter that most were just as innocent as he was – just victims of circumstance. But this was survival of the fittest. Mike's reprieve would last about 90 seconds before the shoving from others forced a repeat scenario. It was grueling for Mike on the inside. I felt guilty. I had the easy task – hit without getting hit, mostly. Others saw the brilliance of our teamwork and before I knew it, I had company on my side of the rail.

Eventually, Mike scored tickets. Battle scarred, Mike more than I, we walked away from the mayhem to the other side of the stadium which was mostly vacant now. We popped my backseat into the car and drove home, elated.

Uh-oh!

I learned a new trick when I was in high school. Put a damp towel across the lower crack of a closed

99

door and Mom and Dad wouldn't know. I had picked up the nasty addiction of smoking.

Anyway, it was late at night. I had to pee before turning in. I knew I'd be quick so instead of snuffing out a perfectly good cigarette, I hung it off the edge of my desk. There was no need to reset the towel, that's how quickly I'd be back.

Returning to my room, I did a face plant into my door. It had locked when it closed. Visions of the burning cigarette falling into the carpeting sent a shiver up my spine. All it would take would be a slight breeze from the open window and I'd be toast – along with the house.

Frantically, I tried to jimmy the door open.

"What are you doing up there," came a loud whisper-voice from my mom. "You're going to wake your father up."

My dad was a light sleeper. He had to wake up at 4:30 a.m. to get ready for work. If I disturbed his sleep, he'd be upset. If he caught me smoking, I would be another statistic chalked up to smoking related deaths. If I caught the house on fire, he would revive me just to kill me again.

I had no choice but to spill the gravity of the situation to my mom.

All of this transpired at light-speed.

The next thing I knew, we were standing in the garage. My mom was in her robe. We hurriedly lifted a massive aluminum extension ladder off the wall and somewhat sprinted – in a wiggly fast walk – to the front of the house. My window overlooked a peak over the front door. On the other side of the front door was my parents' bedroom.

When the aluminum ladder connected with the aluminum gutter on the peak, Mom and I froze and listened for Dad's voice.

Nothing.

"Go-go-go..." Mom hurried me up the ladder.

Halfway up, she yelled in that loud whisper-voice, "Police car!"

I was almost there when I stopped, looked over my shoulder and sure enough, a patrol car was slowly coming down the street, right in the direction of our house.

No doubt we looked like burglars!

My mom ducked into the shrubs. I tried not to laugh out loud.

The police car moved so slowly it was painful. How he did not see me on a big extension ladder scaling the front of my house, glimmering in the street light I'll never know.

I popped out my screen, rolled silently into my room and found a long ash leading to a burned out butt, leaving a heat stain on my desktop.

After all was clear, I chain smoked my nerves back to normal ...outside!

Gore Orphanage

We moved a temporary "bridge out" sign so we could drive our car across. Clearly, the bridge was not out, but we were, for a good time.

We had driven well across rural Lorain County, a route so many teens have come to know. Mike and Bobby had the munchies. We pulled off at a rickety old roadside store and they went inside.

"Look, is that someone leaning out of the window above the store?" asked one of the girls in the backseat.

I rolled the window down.

"Do-o-o-on't go-o," the stranger lobbed down to us.

We looked at each other inside the car. When we looked back up, the stranger in the window was gone.

"What the hell was that?" asked one of the girls sitting behind me.

Surely it was just some guy having fun with us.

Mike and Bobby jumped back in the car. They didn't believe a word out of our mouths about the stranger in the window.

Eventually, we arrived at a desolate country road which led down a steep, narrow hill. We noticed but ignored the "no trespassing" signs riddled with bullet holes. Near the bottom of the hill there was a turn-off to the left that veered so sharply it was difficult to see. This offshoot was even steeper and narrower and led to blackness. Our other option was to continue on the main route and ascend up the other side.

We chose blackness.

With windows rolled down on a crisp night, we listened as we puttered up to "heartbeat bridge."

"Kill the engine!"

We listened. Then, we got out and leaned against the metal bridge.

"I heard it."

"Me too."

"I didn't hear shit."

The legend was that long ago, there was an orphanage that burned to the ground taking with it dozens of kids. If you listened closely, you could hear their faint cries echoing through the valley. Oh, and if you turned your car off on heartbeat bridge, it wouldn't restart until you pushed it off. So, we intentionally left it out of gear to spook the girls. They even gave it a try before we pushed it to the other side. Wouldn't you know it, it started right up. You could probably catch us winking and smirking at each other on the sly if you were looking in the rear-view mirror.

We continued down the all but forgotten road, winding around a bend one way and then back another before pulling over to park.

"They say the foundation of the orphanage is that way," Mike said, pointing a flashlight in the direction of the trailhead, where woods met an open field.

Before going there, we ventured up the road on foot. There was a lonely house at the end of a long wooded driveway.

"Holy crap! Someone lives down here!"

Uphill, around a bend, the road was barricaded. We went back to the car.

"Oh no, cops!"

"Those aren't cops, they're teenagers."

And they led us to the foundation. At the tree line was a lone pillar. Large graffiti warned, "You are now entering Hell."

We sat on the remaining foundation blocks and befriended the new carload of strangers. They decided to leave before us but we weren't far behind.

As they drove away, I went for some kicks. I threw my flashlight as hard as I could, end over end, high over their windshield, freaking them out. They sped off. Pleased with myself, I ran, laughing, to pick up my flashlight. Within minutes, it died. Worse, unbeknownst to me, my car keys bounced out of my unzipped jacket pocket.

We knew we were up shit creek without a paddle after our failed attempts to search for the lost keys. The other flashlight went dead. So, Mike and I left Bobby with the girls and went to the old house to ask for batteries or a flashlight. It was pretty late at night.

A freak rain shower drove down upon us forcing us to return to the car. Everyone bitched up a storm.

"Shut-up!"

"What the …"

We were all staring out of the back window at an old-looking pickup truck pulling off the road near our car.

"Get down."

Peeking over the back seat, we all witnessed a man jump from the truck. He was carrying something long. He let three dogs out the passenger door and they all ran into the field together and out of our sight.

"What do we do?"

POP!

"What the hell was that?"

"Was that a gunshot?"

"Here he comes!"

The man emerged with two dogs, hopped in his truck and motored away.

When we finally peeled ourselves from the floor mats, the rain had stopped. It was past midnight. We were stranded ...far from home.

Amazingly, another vehicle appeared. No, it was two cars carrying more teenagers. They were locals. One agreed to drive me back to his parents' house so I could call my mom. She would have to come out with a spare key.

"Now, listen carefully, Mom. At that point, you'll have to get out and move a sign that says *bridge out* but don't worry, you can cross. Ignore the *no trespassing* signs. Go down the road that looks like a car should not go down. It gets really steep and narrow ..."

It was close to dawn when we got home. But it would be a long time before any of us saw the light of day again.

Is this Mahogany?

There was a chunk of metal lodged in my eyeball. Fortunately it was in the white, barely! Nonetheless, you could see it and it hurt.

It must have happened in metal shop. I thought it was just a bug until I got home and looked in the mirror. I called my mom at work and she made a doctor's appointment for me. The problem was I had to drive to Cleveland. Mom told me to drive to my grandma and grandpa's house and they would give me more detailed directions to the doctor's office from there.

When I got there, Grandma took one look at my eye and said, "You can't drive like that."

She called out to Grandpa, "Cliff, you take him."

My grandpa hated doctors and despised hospitals. Once, I heard a story about how he walked home in a hospital gown. The chances of him agreeing to take me were slim and ..."

"Sure!" he said.

I told him he could wait in the waiting room but he insisted on going in with me. He was in a chair and I was on the examination table.

The nurse came in and took my temperature.

"Take mine too," my grandpa said.

I looked at the nurse, she at Grandpa and he nodded to do it, with puppy dog eyes, so she did. I got my blood pressure tested, Grandpa got his tested and so on and so forth. After each test, he asked how he did. Not how I did but how he did.

The nurse would smile and say, "Ju-u-ust fine."

Grandpa looked pleased with his free checkup.

The nurse left for a while and then came back with the doctor. My grandpa was opening and closing the door, examining it.

"Is this mahogany?" he asked the doctor.

The doctor looked dumbfounded.

"That's good stuff. Nice solid door," Grandpa kept examining it while the doctor examined me.

The doctor and nurse said they had never removed a piece of metal that large from any eye without surgery. They began to explain the risks.

Grandpa walked over, edged past the doctor and looked at my eye.

"Why I see no reason we can't just take it out here and be done with it." Grandpa said that, not the doctor.

Low and behold the doctor agreed.

I about shit myself.

Nightmare on Grove Street

It was very late when I came home so I did as I always did after a night out; I entered the house extra quietly so as not to wake my parents.

I had some serious munchies so I opened the refrigerator door, slowly, so nobody could hear the rubber seal peel apart. Then, I opened and closed the cupboard, softly, so I wouldn't make as much as a peep. The real trick was pouring a big bowl of cereal without the thunderous sound of it hitting the bottom of the bowl. I broke its fall with fingers spread wide on my hand – hardly a rustle. I knew where the creaky floor boards were so I walked the edge of the kitchen into the dining room. I sat cautiously so the swivel seat didn't squeak when I turned and melted into it.

The dining room overlooked the sunken family room. Strange, the television was still on. I ate my cereal slowly, trying not to clank the spoon against the sides of the bowl. I figured someone accidentally left the TV on so, lucky for me, I had entertainment while I enjoyed my late night binge. I quickly became engrossed in the movie – the original Nightmare on Elm Street.

The plot thickened and the tension built. My eyes were glued to the screen. So much so, I bumped my cheeks a few times with a spoon full of heaven as I fumbled for my open mouth. I chewed slowly, creating a mush before I swallowed so the amplified crunching in my ears didn't interfere with hearing the TV.

Something was definitely going to happen soon! There I was, all alone, enjoying my cereal and an intense horror flick for the times. Just as Freddy Krueger, the disfigured serial killer who used a gloved hand with long finger-razors to kill his victims, was about to kill again, the entire family room burst with blood-curdling, girlish screams. It was so sudden and shocking I swung from the chair, took one step to run and met the wall. The next thing I remembered was being spread eagle on my back, looking up, wondering why my face hurt so bad.

From this vantage point, I saw down the two steps between the couch and chair. The floor of the family room was covered with about a dozen 13-year-old girls in sleeping bags. I tried to process the scene. My sister was having a slumber party. Gaining my senses, I was about to slink away, hopefully unnoticed. That's when a silhouette emerged from darkness. Before I could do anything, the shadowy figure of a girl tripped over me.

I panicked and almost jumped through my skin, like having an out of body experience – clearly she experienced the same fright. She shrieked and fell back into the family room, knocking down who-knows-what and startling every girl in the room. I wanted to flee as quickly as I could but I was not that fast in getting up. Apparently my knee wasn't working. It felt like the cap was cracked, it hurt so badly, no doubt from my earlier collision with the wall.

Everyone's attention turned toward the dining room. I slowly stood up in the shadows of the dull light emanating from the television screen. I could feel a wall of terror coming from the girls. As I darted towards the doorway to the kitchen, I miscalculated and went sprawling again. The thud was followed by a moment of silence. I quickly jumped back to my feet and this time found the opening and fled out of their sight.

As I clumsily navigated through the kitchen to run upstairs, I heard frantic voices, "What was that? …Who was that? …I want out of here! …Turn off the TV! …Linda, was that your brother?"

Skinny Dipping Dips

Growing up a stone's throw from Lake Erie provided many good times.

Common watery pastimes included fishing, although I never really enjoyed it as much as my family and friends. What I did enjoy was being a bum all summer long at Huntington Beach. We'd throw Frisbee, hit on girls, play Hacky Sack and dive for footballs that we lobbed into waves. When the waves got really big, it was pure joy to flip your entire body haphazardly into them. Staying up all night and swimming at sunrise was right up there, too.

Huntington closed at night but we'd park and walk there. I used to enjoy taking girls to sit out on the roof of a storage shack on the beach. If you got on the other side of the railing, it was a short jump to the shingles. We'd lie back on the lake side under the stars, listening to the soft rippling waves, out of sight from foot patrols. We'd have to be quiet, which was always my plan anyway.

Another favorite pastime was floating away the hours on old inner tubes. They weren't store bought. They usually came, used, from a grandparent's garage. At least that's where mine came from. My grandpa made his living retreading tires. Anyway, we'd ride bicycles to Veteran's Memorial Park, one handed with old car tire inner tubes hung over our neck and a shoulder. They were big, black and usually had one spot that bulged so you could lean against it for more comfort. But you had to position away from that damn valve. Another nuisance was flipping the black rubber inner tube every so often when the sun made it too hot to touch. Nothing was better than this except for skinny dipping with girls, but that rarely happened. In fact, that was about as rare as catching a fish from the shore in January …unless you were behind the power plant.

One hot summer night, Pete and I were sitting on the embankment of the old cemetery facing Lake Erie next to what we called the boat club. We were just kicked back, enjoying the cool breeze and mist coming from the water, trying to bend each other's brain with conversation we thought was trippy. It was a great way to enjoy a summer night in Avon Lake. Only one thing could top it and they appeared from behind us, giggling.

So we sat with two girls, one was from out of town, visiting the other. That was always a good thing because they were looking for thrills to

110

remember the visit. We were thrill seekers, so they happened upon the right guys.

After about a half an hour of warming them up with chatter and laughter, they beat us to the punch.

We couldn't believe our own ears when they said, nearly in tandem, "Do you want to go skinny dipping?"

We were half unclothed, walking to the break wall pier before they even finished their sentences.

"Hell yah, let's go," we said, pausing to look back.

"You first and then we'll come," said the townie.

"Shy?" we laughed.

"A little. This is our first time so you go, then we'll come. Turn the other way when you get in the water and count to 10 out loud and we'll be there," the townie insisted.

There were no more questions from us – just counting.

When we got to 10, they weren't with us. We looked up the shore trying to see them but they weren't there. We looked at each other and back up the shore again, this time calling out.

There was no answer.

"What the …?"

We got out, buck naked, and looked for the last garments we had cast aside but they were gone.

"Ahhh, hell noooo…!"

It hit us. We'd been had! They stole our clothes.

We left coolness in the lake and pleaded to the night air for our clothes back. Our requests went unanswered. By this time, we were at our original spot and continued to plead with the night. Eventually, our pleas turned to realization and desperation. What the heck were we to do? We didn't drive or ride here. We walked at least a mile.

"Dude, what are we going to do?" Pete asked.

The humor of our predicament didn't escape me so I had to laugh, albeit an uneasy laugh.

"We're screwed!" I said.

There was no way we could even attempt crossing Lake Road buck naked without being noticed. That's when we heard a giggle from the cemetery. We went to investigate and plea some more. Pete's voice grew in anger as he now knew they were listening.

So, there we were, playing a naked game of cat and mouse, running around a cemetery trying to free at least some shorts from these evil temptresses.

"I got a sock!" I yelled to Pete.

"Who's is it?" Pete yelled back.

"Mine," I said even though I couldn't tell.

One by one, we completed the unwilling scavenger hunt laid out by the temptresses. Eventually, we even got the girls. But we never got their clothes off.

Skiing

Mike was "Mr. Ski Club." We stood atop a hill at Brandywine ready for the first run of the day for him and my first run ever.

He was checking down with all that I needed to know and I just ya-ya'd him, impatient and ready to go.

Finally, I said, "Got it!" And shot downhill like a bullet.

I heard, "But ..." and nothing else as my friend's voice faded.

I sailed so fast over the snow, straight down the hill, that I freaked out. I could not turn, stop or even slow down!

As I bore down on a man skiing up ahead, I cringed. He crisscrossed effortlessly, kicking up powdery white stuff. I was sure he was going to be knocked from here to eternity when I collided with him in about two seconds flat.

Why didn't I stick around to listen to Mike explain how to turn, or better yet, how to stop?

As others described later, it looked like I was shot out of canon and about to kill somebody. They watched from above in horror, waiting for my impact with this unsuspecting stranger. Precisely at the very last moment, everyone closed their eyes or took a deep breath, and I *woosh-wooshed* around the man. In two quick movements with my feet, I skirted disaster – barely. My friends said the guy stood straight up, shocked by the brush back but was otherwise uninterrupted.

When I got near the bottom, I managed to wipe myself out to stop along a flat straightaway.

Mike came down the hill like a pro. This was baby stuff to him. Near the bottom, he hit a raised area to get fancy in the air. When he came down, he injured his ankle. Go figure.

Later in the day, the guys either thought I was ready for the meanest slope at the resort or were willing to see me die for laughs. As the saying goes, with friends like these, who needs enemies?

The ski lift got to the top but I was snagged and couldn't shift myself to get off. The chair turned and rose higher off the ground, circling the control shack at the top. I mentally foreshadowed the humiliation of returning to the bottom of the slope, alone on a chair lift.

NO WAY!

I flung my body in a pathetic but successful last attempt to free myself. The problem was that I was not as close to the ground anymore but I landed on my feet, and then fell to my butt with quite a thud.

The lift stopped and a guy popped his operating shack door open yelling, "You alright?"

Laughing uncomfortably, I said, "Ya."

He laughed, said "crazy," shook his head, shut the door and started the lift again.

Looking downhill, it was clear that this course was not for beginners. In fact, it looked wickedly dangerous for someone like me. My depth perception was off. The slope was laden in terrain characterized by a large number of different bumps, or moguls. Not only that, but this slope was the steepest by far. Much like the beginning of the day, I became a human, heat-seeking missile.

Unlike earlier in the day, these moguls posed a different experience altogether. Quickly, my knees vibrated violently up and down at high speed. I should have wiped out, but instead I found myself lying straight on my back but upright on the skis. I could see the lift chairs overhead, off to the side, even though my head bounced violently off the never-ending moguls.

From my friends' perspective, when my skis finally turned in on each other and I wiped out, it was like a scene from "The Agony of Defeat," which was an infamous ski jumping sports clip gone oh-so-wrong. When I tumbled, it was bad. My body looked like a rag doll plummeting down the slope amidst an avalanche of snow and debris. By everyone's account, they thought I broke every bone in my body. I lost both skis, poles, one boot and the other had every buckle burst open.

Mike was the first to get to me. "He's conscious!"

The others gathered my stuff strewn all over the slope.

It was all we could talk about the rest of the evening as everyone recalled, in vivid detail, my spectacular flight down the slope. The laughter roared like the fire we perched in front of with hot cocoa.

I never skied again.

Fire in the Art Room

Our high school art room was once the gymnasium well before our time. It still had a parquet wood floor. A couple of smaller rooms were walled off from the main spread, which was huge for an art room. On one side of the big room was a long and deep balcony and on the other was an elevated glass-walled office and storage area. Both sides previously served as seating for sporting events.

Art classes spanned two study periods, scheduled at the end of the day, so we were in this room for huge blocks of time. After instructions for the day, the art teacher allowed us free rein to set up and let our creativity flow. Our creativity flowed upstairs, out of sight, in the balcony. Its only access was one set of steps other than a locked door to a second story hallway. Along the length of the balcony was a half-wall you could look over to view the big room below. There was a group of four of us who claimed the balcony as our space to work. Eddie, a very gifted artist, would take out the hall pass and skip most of class.

One day, Bobby and I sat in the privacy of the balcony along with Sarah. Bobby and I had finished our projects, so now we just leaned against the wall and talked. He kept putting a glob of rubber cement on a brush stick, dancing it in front of my face, goofing off. I flicked a lighter – jokingly – to ward off the glob before it dripped on me. We were just fooling around and never intended for anything to happen.

The lighter flame, although not touching the glob of rubber cement, somehow ignited it. Both of us snapped into action. Bobby shoved the brush stick lid back onto the jar thinking it would smother it. Instead, it exploded all over the balcony. Little fires were everywhere – on the floor and wall. Sarah, still working away on her project, also sprang into action and scrambled to contain and extinguish the mini fires burning near her.

Just as our frenzy was peaking, Eddie wandered up the stairs. Halfway up, there was a landing and a turn. He was nonchalant, pausing briefly to take in the crazy scene.

Our eyes met.

He turned away saying, "I had nothing to do with this!"

I bolted downstairs to get water. Just as I hit the lower floor, the teacher appeared across the room. My racing body caught his attention. He looked up so I slowed to a very casual pace, flipped the faucet on and filled a container of water. He looked away. I casually gazed up, heart pounding, expecting to see smoke curdling over the top of the balcony but there wasn't any. I walked normally halfway up the steps but as soon as I was out of view from the floor below, I leapt to the top in time to help douse the last of the fires.

The main fire was much bigger and in the middle of the carpeted floor. Bobby had used a pile of old art projects, out of desperation, to smash it out. It all melted into a collage of glue, cardboard and carpet. It left an obvious and hideous black spot. Just then, the "tone" as we referred to it, sounded over the P.A. system. It signaled the change of class periods or in this case, the last bell.

We scrambled to hide our mess. We located a razor blade knife and cut out a section of carpet buried under old looms stuffed deep in a corner of the balcony. Then we cut out the large charred spot in the middle of the carpet, rolled it up and stuffed it inside one of the huge old looms. With little time, we decided to scatter a bunch of stuff over the top of the "hole" and finish our cover-up the next day. We figured nobody came up there but us, anyway.

The next day came and every time a class changed, gossip about the art room spread like wildfire. Police showed up. Every class was interrogated. During lunch, Bobby and I sneaked up the balcony stairs to see what was up. Our cover-up attempt was not only uncovered, revealing the hole we left, but markers were put everywhere our little fires had burned on the floor and walls. Around the perimeter of the big hole was the unrolled charred section of carpet we had cut out, a lighter, rubber cement bottle — or what was left of one side — and other things that were damning to us.

It frightened us. This was a crime scene!

As the end of the day approached, Eddie, Sarah and others in the know passed Bobby and I in the halls during class changes saying things like, "You are screwed ...It was nice knowing you ...The cops are grilling everyone from every class."

We felt the heat closing in and decided to come clean, voluntarily, to see if that might help alleviate the hellfire that was sure to rain down on us. Promptly, we were sent to the vice principal's office.

When we walked up to the desk in the main office and told the secretary what we were there for, she got up, walked past us and said, "I am not sticking around to see this!"

We looked at each other, puzzled, and took a seat to wait for our sentencing. We waited and waited for what seemed to be an eternity and then the vice principal walked in. He looked at us, confused, and asked where the secretary went. Then he asked what we were waiting for. We said we were the ones who burnt up the art room.

"IN MY OFFICE – NOW!"

He slammed the door behind us and began to ream us good – and I mean GOOD! Blood vessels were popping in his beat-red neck and face.

Somewhere in the tirade, I raised my hand saying, "But, but, but …"

I wanted him to know we came forward on our own hoping for some mercy. It was the only card we had to play.

He stopped and shouted, "BUT WHAT!"

I told him. He paused. Silently, for a split moment, he contemplated in his mind on how to proceed. And just as we had hoped, he respected our voluntary admission, switching from a rage to a lecture. He let us off with seven detentions each – no suspension. We couldn't believe our ears.

And our parents couldn't believe the carpet bill.

Chank

A group of us planned to go to Cedar Point, otherwise known as the best amusement park on the planet.

The morning came and we managed to track down everyone scattered around town wherever last night's parties dispensed them. This was before cell phones. The gang was eventually retrieved by word-of-mouth.

On the road to fun, we decided to pull off and get smokes and candy. Nobody was in the store, not even the clerk. We had what we needed and quickly grew impatient, waiting. We paused and yelled out for service one last time. Even though we were halfway through a heist, I think we secretly wanted someone to show up. Well, maybe not all of us. "Shark" had already made two trips to the truck.

It was a scalding hot day so we found ourselves in the longest line in the park, waiting for a water ride. We stood, walked a few feet and stood some more, over and over like zombies. Bored, we came up with our own entertainment as the line snaked slowly along the maze of railings. We told one of our friends that if he yelled "Chank" at the top of his lungs 100 times, we'd jump into the pond when we neared it. Chank was a slang word we used for an ugly woman.

"Really?"

"Yes, really."

"CHANK-CHANK-CHANK..."

We were doubled over, laughing – howling laughing. People were trapped in line and had to deal with it. The people behind us left a big gap in the line.

"...CHANK-CHANK-CHANK...   50!
...CHANK-CHANK-CHANK..."

His voice was going hoarse, but he kept belting it out. We couldn't believe it. This was really happening. He was hell bent on getting to a hundred.

"CHANK-CHANK-CHANK... 100! ...Jump in guys!"

"No way!"

We didn't budge. It was an awful betrayal. We never imagined the possibility of the impossible happening. And there was nothing our friend could do about it but get angry ...very, very angry.

Tension built, even on the water ride. When it made the final turn and floated against the slowly spinning, giant platform where riders exited and new riders boarded, things erupted. If we weren't jumping in the pond, he was going to make sure we at least got wetter than we already were. He hung halfway out of our boat and splashed us with everything he could muster. Eddie exited left, into the water, and splashed back. The water fight escalated when we all abandoned ship. We were maniacs splashing and dunking each other in the water as other boats and riders slowly crept by, some laughing at us and some horrified by the scene. Park workers flocked to us and eventually got our attention.

We were removed from the ride but to our astonishment, not from the park.

Party Central

There were several party houses during my high school days but my best friend's was party central – at least for our crew. His parents were RV enthusiasts and we always reassembled the house cleaner than we found it before they'd return. Call it self-preservation and planning ahead.

One Friday, I was called out of class because there was a death in my family and my dad was coming to pick me up in front of the school. I waited, very concerned wondering which grandparent passed. A huge RV rolled up in front of me in the bus lane. It was my friend, Mike.

"Get in!"

"What the hell, man?" I couldn't believe my eyes. "What are you doing?"

"Picking you up!"

"Dude, my dad's on his way. Someone ..."

"I know, hop in sonny," he interrupted.

Here, he had skipped school (and he was the honor student) because his parents went on a trip without the RV. He grew bored so he pretended to be my dad and called the school, staging the whole hoax. I laughed, somewhat in shock at the magnitude of this, jumped in and didn't look back.

Crazy stuff happened at Mike's house on a regular basis. His dad had an amazing collection of World War II artifacts, mainly weaponry. So, there was the night our other best friend, Steve (we were three peas in a pod), was shaken from a heart-wrenching break-up. Three sheets to the wind, he answered the knock at the door dressed in full combat gear, rounds of ammunition dripping off his torso, Kevlar helmet and rifle. Fortunately the policeman had a sense of humor and sense of understanding. The fact he knew Steve's father may have also helped. That said, it was understood that we needed to heed his warning to turn down the music and not force him to come back.

If you fell asleep at one of these parties, that was your mistake. It wasn't uncommon for someone to wake up in the morning missing some hair or having black magic marker writing all over their face.

Anyway, this particular night had all of the usual mischief and more.

I had to bring my car home for the night but was allowed to sleep over Mike's house. Although he lived halfway across town, I walked. Two other friends came with me. Halfway down Electric Boulevard, a police cruiser pulled up and cut off our path on the sidewalk. The officer got out and began questioning us. It was more like accusations than questions but we had done nothing wrong – not illegally wrong anyway – not outside my friend's house anyway.

"There was vandalism …" the officer continued.

My mom always told me to have no fear if you did nothing wrong. So, I stayed calm whereas my two buddies were itchy nervous to my side, I could sense it.

"Sir, where did this vandalism happen?" I asked.

Dad always taught me to be polite and respectful in such situations – okay maybe he was referring to being faced with a simple speeding ticket but I applied the advice more broadly.

The officer mentioned a neighborhood far from where we stood and not even close to being in the path from my house to my friend's. I explained our whereabouts and said he could even verify it with my parents as we just left there not too long ago.

He got steamed. I recognized that I had seen this hot-headed cop before, so I walked on egg shells and tried to cooperate with his roadside interrogation.

"When did it happen, sir?" I asked.

"Last night," he said matter of fact.

I couldn't believe my ears and let my emotions flow out unchecked; justified by wrongful accusation, witch hunting, railroading or whatever you want to call it.

"Why stop and try to blame us for something that happened last night way over there?" I asked, losing my cool.

My friends took a step back, I presumed due to the street light now in my eyes.

"You're a fucking vandal is what you are," the officer said very angrily.

He slipped off his gun belt and held it off to his side and said, "Let's see what you got – you think you're so damn tough!"

I processed the obvious real quick. I was either going to get pummeled into oblivion or if by some miracle, I got lucky and somehow licked him, I'd be jail-bound for a good long time. Lose – lose: That was my situation.

"I meant no disrespect, sir. I was merely defending myself trying to point out what seems to me as very unlikely and undeserving for us to be questioned for this," I struggled to speak fast, trying to choose the right words to diffuse this lunatic.

"Just as I thought, you're just a pussy," he said putting his belt back on.

He got in his cruiser and left us.

My friends were still speechless as we resumed walking. When they did start talking, they never shut up and by the time we got back to party central a legend was in the making.

Although my status amongst peers grew overnight, I was alarmed at what had happened so the next day I did what any fearful boy would do – I told my mom. She was appalled and called the police station but nothing ever became of it.

Mohican

The times we had along the banks of the Mohican River in high school and college days were for the ages.

The first time a bunch of us got permission from our parents to go on a one-week camping trip to Mohican State Park, it was Easter break. On our first night, we submerged our beer supply in the river and tied it off to a tree in case rangers stopped by. They did late that night and made us pour out what we had around the fire pit.

Close by, someone else had another "party favor" and tossed it into a tent. It hit someone in the head, waking them from their sound sleep. They in turn whipped the object back out, unbeknownst to the rest of us. One of the rangers stumbled on it, as he walked around with his flashlight, examining the area.

"Well what have we here?" the ranger asked out loud, motioning to his partner.

Our jaws dropped. They put the heat on us to give up the rest of the stash. Panic ensued and everything was turned over, except the week supply of beer under water. Fortunately, only a few of us were clued in on that and we weren't cracking under pressure. The rangers took us to a pay phone and made us all call home to say we would be kicked out of the park and returning in the morning. And that's what half the group did – the half that actually called home.

The group of us who stayed hunted for a new campsite outside of the state park boundaries. We found the perfect spot. For the rest of the week, we enjoyed our freedom and even the company of a stray dog we took in.

Tyler made a run to score supplies. When he pulled up to the campsite, Tommy ran out to greet him, jumping onto the hood of the truck. He miscalculated the speed of the truck and sailed over the hood and into the windshield, "spider webbing" the glass.

We deemed it safer to just tear out the whole windshield so we did.

"People will just think that the glass is super clean."

On the drive home, Tommy occasionally stretched his legs out of the truck cabin onto the hood. It was a funny and bizarre sight.

A tradition took root as did the folklore surrounding our escapades from year-to-year. Our Mohican crew grew considerably. One year in particular, it was a rainy and muddy experience. Most tents washed away the first night but we survived. Due to our group size, the campground had us in a wide open field, shared by a much larger group adjacent to us. One afternoon, we decided to challenge them to a football game.

They smiled and asked, "Touch or tackle?"

We smiled back and said, "Tackle of course."

They grimaced and said, "We better play touch."

We walked away laughing under breath.

As we gathered our team – half our players already in the tank with the motto, "It's gotta be Noon somewhere" – a small band of girls came from the other campsite to tell us we're lucky it's going to be a touch football game.

We sneered and asked, "Ya, why's that?"

"Because they are the best football players from around the state and just wrapped up a football camp."

It turned out that they were just taking precautions to reduce the chances of getting injured.

We walked to the field of play. Their players stretched, ours were only working out one arm doing bends with bottle to mouth. Their sideline had cheerleaders – honest to goodness cheerleaders doing cheers! Our women hauled coolers to our side of the field.

For a touch football game, it was arguably the most physically demanding football game I had ever played. They were killing us! By halftime, the expectations changed for both sides. We just wanted to score once. And they knew if that happened, it would be considered a loss by their standards.

Then, there it was. A 15-yard-pass by our opponent over the middle and Justin leapt into the air making a one-handed interception while holding a beer in his other hand. He landed running, never spilling a drop! The miracle of the gridiron continued. He made moves his body should not have been able to do. Then, he streaked downfield – untouched – an entire team hot on his heels. Justin had no blockers. We were all on the ground laughing at the impossibility unraveling before our eyes. He scored and our sideline became soaked in a beer shower.

The pandemonium wouldn't cease so the other team walked away. You could hear their discontent.

Some argued to the point that they nearly fist-fought each other.

In our last year of this ongoing tradition and annual reunion of sorts, the planning for the size of our party started nearly a year in advance. The early planning allowed us to reserve multiple sites grouped together back down by the river, given cover by trees. It was raucous to say the least. We would put sparklers in the hands of someone sleeping outside and take pictures and make mischief into the wee hours of morning.

Then, when only a handful of us — trying to pull an all-nighter — were gathered, conversationally, around the fire, Tommy shattered the quiet of the night, "You gotta come now and check this out!"

What could it be? We were in the middle of nowhere and it was so late and dark.

Coming out of the tree line, we saw a rather large, orange glow coming from atop a hill on the far side of the open field.

"What the ..."

Then, an eerie silence fell around us. We stood speechless at a sight we never could have imagined: A towering wooden cross, burning, with white hooded people around it. They were wrapped in full Ku Klux Klan garb — some of the design work was hauntingly elaborate.

"H-H-H-H-o-l-y shhh..!"

I just remember feeling a sense of fear. Seeing such hate first-hand really hit me.

When the police came — finally — some of us cheered. I think others wanted to but didn't want to call attention over to them. The law's presence allowed us the courage to walk straight up to the haters for a closer look.

That night was a buzz kill because the officers only arrested a couple of people and had the cross extinguished and taken down. The rest of the Klan got to stay, albeit in street clothes!

We wondered about our cheers, their looks and thus pulling an all-nighter became a breeze.

Golden Boy

As a little kid, my hair used to get platinum blond in summer. Mom called me her golden boy. In my teens, my hair was still light but it took the summer sun to bleach it blond.

Near the tail end of my senior year of high school, I got a bright idea. I'd speed up nature and bring the summer blond in early with a little help. Understand I was a tee shirt and jeans kind of guy that basically didn't put much thought into style, except for maybe wearing a rolled bandana around my head covered mostly by my hair. Oh, and the parachute pants phase. But, I had an idea and when I got an idea, I rolled with it for better or worse.

I was in a total women's aisle at the grocery store looking at hair products. Self-conscious, I picked one quickly and drove home. Mom applied the product and we both neglected to read where it said to avoid direct sunlight.

"Go sit out on the patio in case that stuff drips," Mom advised.

The instructions said something about letting it set for 15 minutes so I figured longer would be

129

even better. I chilled outside on the back patio, shirtless and barefoot, wearing Bermuda shorts and Wayfarer sunglasses – hair full of suds.

I had an image in mind, nothing drastic, just a subtle shade lighter to get that beach-bum look going for me. Okay, maybe I was hoping for two shades lighter. Prom was just around the corner.

When the timer went off, I sat a while longer just to make sure it took. Then, I went to the bathroom to wash it all out and marvel at my perfection. Our downstairs bathroom was dark, especially as my eyes adjusted from outside, despite having had sunglasses on. I rubbed a towel around my head. My hair was semi-long so I knew the waves in it would be cool with some highlights.

I looked straight into the mirror and my jaw dropped!

My hair glowed! It was fluorescent blond. If such a thing didn't exist, I just invented it.

"M-O-O-O-OMMM!"

I walked out to the kitchen and she turned around and had a combined reaction of horror and humor twisted together in her eye-popping, ear-piercing, "Oh-my-goodness. What happened!" as she tried to contain her laughter.

Every five minutes, I'd look in different mirrors in the house only to see the same stark sight. Then, I'd stare at it for four minutes, take a minute to find another mirror and stare again. No words could make me feel better. I knew I was doomed. If ever there was a moment I wanted to die or at least drop out of school, this was it.

"I can't go to school like this!" I shouted.

"Don't be silly, it'll be just fine," Mom said, lying through her teeth.

We came up with a solution. Short spiked hair was kind of stylish at the time so I ran up to the neighborhood barber shop. I hadn't been there in years.

The crowd and conversation were the same other than the comments, "What the hell did you do?" ..."I'll need sunglasses to cut this," ..."This new generation, I tell ya..."

I came home a hair better albeit spiked and fluorescent.

Going to school the following Monday was one of the most difficult things I ever had to do. Oh, there were definitely double-takes and finger pointing. I was eye-catching to say the least when all I really wanted was to be invisible. Regardless, I decided to wear my new look loud and proud – trying to convince myself and others that this was the outcome I had intended.

A week later, humbled, I walked into school and down the main hallway. As I looked around, I began to see sunspots. I blinked and tried to clear my eyes but I still saw sun spots dancing amongst the heads of other students. As I passed a kid coming from the opposite direction, he said hi. He wore a proud smile along with his fluorescent, blond, spiked hair! I couldn't believe my eyes. I stopped in my tracks, turned to watch him walking away, stunned as to what I just saw. What made it worse was his hair and complexion were much darker than mine, normally, and he was much taller so he REALLY stood out. It was obvious he and –

as fate would have it – a couple of others, did this purposefully.

I scratched my fluorescent head, confused.

North Point

A teenager from the neighborhood died cliff jumping. Rumor was that he was night jumping with friends and never came up. So, the police cracked down on this pastime of ours. Still, it was hard to stop doing something we'd always done.

North Point was our favorite place to cliff jump. There was a little road snaking the edge of a cliff along the Lake Erie shoreline. The road had been closed at times to reinforce a retaining wall used to stop the street from caving in due to erosion. The retaining wall was made of a wavy metal allowing Eddie – it was always Eddie – to scale down to the lake, swim out to our landing area, which was further out on the point, and test the depth of the water. He determined if it was deep enough that we wouldn't be crippled when we plunged forcefully to the lake floor. This took a while.

When he returned, he gave the thumbs up. Then, he said he needed to take a leak. There was a vacant overgrown lot across the way so he went behind some brush. When he finished, he was headed back when an older lady appeared on a nearby porch, yelling at him. Eddie looked back at her, pretended to be flustered and ran straight off the cliff waving his hands in the air, screaming. I looked at the older woman and could read shock in her body even at that distance. I don't know if she even noticed the rest of us. When she sat down on her front step the way she did, I knew Eddie had scrambled her brain but good. She grasped the railing, pulled up and scampered inside.

We figured enough time had passed for Eddie to get up against the cliff so we could jump. We spread out and all went at once before the lady came back.

Something about that jump never got old. You always anticipated hitting the water before you actually got there. Sometimes you experienced the anticipation twice before hitting, but that was usually in the dark. Plus, in the dark, you were subject to whiplash because you had no bearings at all. I suspected that's how that teenager died. He must have been knocked unconscious.

At the bottom, we all whooped it up giving Eddie a play-by-play of what just happened with the older lady, expressions and all. He ate it up.

Some scaled the retaining wall to see if the coast was clear to jump again. Others, myself included, decided to swim and float on rafts. When we first arrived, we had tossed our water toys over the edge of the cliff.

By the time the climbers reached the top, breathless from the ascent, two squad cars greeted them. I was in a raft with one of the girls. She wanted to flee the scene, but a policeman was calling to us through a megaphone. So, I paddled in and we climbed up, only to get cited for criminal trespassing.

It was close to my 18th birthday so I was tried as an adult. It was also close to my reporting date to begin basic training in the U. S. Army.

The prosecutor scared the shit out of me. He was definitely a man on a mission and that mission was to hang me out to dry. I was the first to be tried for this particular offense so my case would set a critical precedent.

"We have to send a strong message so nobody does this again!" declared the prosecutor.

Loaded for bear, he meant business and lambasted me. I just stood before the judge – silent.

Then, I got a turn to talk. I had no representation. I had a court date to show up, so that's what I did, alone.

"I'm going into the Army in a couple of weeks. We were just swimming where we had our whole lives."

With that, the judge dismissed the case and I was free to go.

The prosecutor lost his mind.

I didn't know what to do from there so I did what came natural and approached the bench with a humbled manner and voice, "Thank you, sir."

The judge just stared at me so I walked away thinking I should have said, your honor. The whole time, the prosecutor continued ranting and raving.

I bolted out the courthouse doors and entered adulthood.

CHAPTER 3:
BEING ALL I COULD BE IN THE
UNITED STATES ARMY

Toe Jam

Stretched out on the lower bunk, I ran my fingers through my fresh crew cut to get that tingly sensation. I already missed home.

In-processing was complete. In the morning, I would be packed into a cattle car and hauled up to Tank Hill to begin basic-training. I felt alone. Next to me were half a dozen new recruits who came together from inner-city Hartford. They were rapping and laughing. My luck, I had the rowdiest bunch clustered on a bunk next to mine. I just wanted to get a good night's sleep knowing it would be the last for two months.

"Shit! …shit-shit-shit," shouted one of my rowdy neighbors.

He bounced around a few times on one foot, clutching the other with his hands before losing his balance and sprawling onto the lower bunk across from me. He had been dancing around showing off his rapping skills and stubbed his toe on the metal frame of the bunk.

"We should call you Toe Jam," I said, casually rolling over.

The place went dead silent. I quickly took note of what I just said and couldn't believe my own ears. The silence was deafening, the stares pierced straight through me and the pause was nine-months pregnant. I was on the verge of getting my ass kicked. Why didn't I mind my own business and keep my mouth shut?

"TOE JAM?" The silence was broken by the guy still holding his foot in pain.

Lying there on my side, acting as nonchalant as I could, I was ready to spring into action.

"I like it!" he said with a grin.

The tension in the room broke so fast you could almost hear the air gushing from a balloon. And just like that, I was part of their circle.

He proudly introduced himself from that day forward as, "...but you can call me Toe Jam."

And every time, I would see the person he just met, pause and process this peculiar nickname.

I wonder if he ever put "toe-and-two" together to realize what else toe jam meant.

The Gas Chamber

We were marched out to a clearing in the woods. There before us stood a non-descript building. It was the size of a modest ranch house, maybe half that or somewhere in between.

There's nothing like the fear of the unknown, unless the fear is known.

We went from bad to worse as soon as we were told, "At ease!"

"Welcome to the gas chamber!" shouted a drill sergeant.

Even the toughest wore faces of uncertainty.

Quickly, the ranks filled with a murmur of questions and answers: "Do they really gas us? ...With what? ...How bad is it?"

One group at a time put on their MOPP gear to prepare to enter. MOPP (Mission Oriented Protective Posture) is a head-to-toe protective gear used in the Army in toxic environments such as chemical warfare. It includes gloves, pants, jacket, and gas mask with hood. We had spent hours in training to get it pulled over our BDUs (Battle Dress Uniforms) in seconds flat once a signal was given. Sometimes we wore it for hours in the blistering, August, South Carolina heat. Usually, when we were about to pass out, we got the all-clear sign.

We were in a line parallel to the rear of the building so those of us in the back of the line could see the first group coming out, one by one, victims. Some yelled, a couple puked, but most just groaned and flapped their arms in the air as tears streamed from their burning eyes. With this haunting imagery set against the thick woods, it was like watching a horror movie unfold. Anyway, it begged the question; would it be better to go in oblivious to the outcome or see the agony of those going first? Some wondered, what's the purpose of having to go through this? I figured the answer was probably so we'd understand just how real this threat was in modern warfare. Granted, the gas used in training was not life-threatening, but it did make your skin and eyes feel like they were burning up.

"Forward, ma-a-a-rch!"

I entered with my group, in full MOPP gear. The first thing that went through my mind was that I hoped every zipper and fastener was sealed properly. We stood in three different lines and one-by-one walked up to a drill sergeant. I was struck by how clear it was inside. It looked plain and harmless. I thought, seriously, how bad could it be?

The first three were ordered to remove their gas masks then walk out the door. It was funny watching them turn stupid all of a sudden. They bumped this way and that way, feeling in front of them as if they were trying to escape a dark room. Of the sets of three, there was usually one who seemed to have little trouble, probably because he pre-planned his route. Then there was one who probably tried to pre-plan but found it more difficult to carry out. And the typical third one never even contemplated it, with fear probably being his foremost thought. One, in particular, actually bumbled around, bumped back into a drill sergeant, and walked into the corner of the room where there was no door to escape.

It was excruciating to watch this. Many of us, me included, wanted to break rank and lead him back in the right direction. The drill sergeants seemed to be enjoying this inept soldier's "malfunctioning" moment. Finally, even they showed mercy, and walked him out with assistance.

When it was my turn, I had already pre-counted the number of steps to the door and had an idea of what angle I needed to take to find it. As soon as I unmasked, the searing pain tore into me. My skin was burning from the get-go. Even closed, my eyes felt like they were incinerated to nothing. I held my breath but the scalding was through and through. I had no idea of how many pre-counted steps or where in this fiery pit of hell I'd find the door. But, I did – and not a moment too soon!

When I exited, I knew it because the fresh air was anything but. I flapped my arms and walked and walked, feeling fried and nauseous. Through my gasping, wheezing and choking, soon I returned back to normal, except for one thing – I had been gassed.

It was a rite of passage. We sat in the grass, later, eating lunch, already reminiscing about our "war" stories.

Grenade!

It was another sweltering hot August day in South Carolina so we were glad to be in the shade of a nearby pavilion. The line snaked like one at an amusement park. The thrill here was practicing throwing hand grenades. This was in preparation for the real deal.

Even though this was serious shit we were learning, it was fun and games to me. I loved shooting the M16, M60 and M72-LAW, which was a Light Anti-Tank Weapon. It was basically a shoulder mounted rocket launcher.

You had to make sure you yelled, "Back blast area clear," so you didn't kill someone walking behind you when you fired it.

So, next on my checklist of cool things I could say I did, once, was throwing a live hand grenade. The training for this was pretty intense. There was a sergeant with facial scars rumored to have had been inflicted when a recruit panicked and dropped a grenade after pulling the pin instead of throwing it. Understandably, there was a fear factor for the drill sergeants having to instruct and shadow untrustworthy recruits in how to throw a live grenade out of a foxhole.

First, we had to practice with dummy grenades. A dirt ring behind some sandbags was used to emulate the foxhole. One by one, we moved up, went through the proper procedure, threw the grenade and moved on. As I snaked through the wooden maze and came to the frontline of the shelter, I had a clear visual of the guys ahead. As I watched them going through the motions with fake grenades, something strange seemed to be happening. Guys were nervous to join the three sergeants, each one waiting in a dirt circle. These were regular sergeants, not drill sergeants. When recruits threw their grenade, the sergeants were having fun slamming them to the ground afterward. It was clearly excessive and they were egging each other on. One recruit shrieked when he hit the ground, pile driven by one of the sergeants. He soon disappeared, supposedly to seek medical attention or his drill sergeant.

The chatter in the pavilion grew and I watched in horror at the abuse unfolding before my eyes. Guys were getting hurt. I don't remember what I yelled other than my disapproval at the sergeant whose line I was in. It was spontaneous and it was regrettable as soon as the words left my lips. He spun around. I was surprised he made out what I said to him as there was some distance and noise between us. I was even more surprised that he pinpointed me in the crowd of camouflage. I almost crapped my pants when he pointed at me and basically said I was a dead man when he got his hands on me.

Fortunately, I was speaking for the masses and they had my back. As soon as the sergeant turned around to body slam the next guy throwing a grenade, I was shuffled through the crowd of recruits to the far side. Now, I was two lines removed from that sergeant. After each guy moved along, that sergeant scanned the line for me. Meanwhile, the other two sergeants were also body slamming guys, unnecessarily. When my turn came, speed was my name. I simultaneously whipped the grenade away while whipping my own body to the ground. Still, the sergeant managed to pile drive his elbow into my shoulder blade but it didn't hurt ...until later. I had too much adrenaline pumping at the time and was relieved I was not recognized.

While I was waiting under a nearby tree for the rest of our guys to finish with this station, a jeep pulled up and brass jumped out. They went straight for the three asshole sergeants. There was hell to pay, especially considering the number of witnesses who bravely stepped forward to attest to what was going on in great detail. The guy who disappeared for medical attention had a broken arm. Justice was served for all to see and it was sweet!

Days later, I was standing in a different line. In this exercise, after each person moved into a fortressed off zone, shrapnel would shower against an adjoining wall we were behind. When it was my turn, I moved to my foxhole, which was built up with sandbags. The feeling was surreal. It felt like slow motion. I pulled the pin and held the safety clip until I was told to throw my grenade. I threw it mightily and paused ever so slightly wanting to see it explode. My stupidity surprised even me. Thankfully, in that split second, the sergeant monitoring me drove me to the ground.

When we got up and dusted off, he merely yelled,
"Next!"

The Disease

Amid the heat, the drills, the lack of sleep, a heady
bunch of kids were being torn down so Uncle Sam
could build us back up – his way!

We had no weekend passes, no television, no
anything. We could stand in a two hour line to call
home from a phone booth on Sundays but I never
did. I could crank out letters to everyone in that
time. Although tensions would bring some to
fisticuffs from time to time, we became tight.

Several platoons joined for a road march to go sit
in classes assembling and disassembling M16s or
whipping on MOPP gear – gas mask and all, in
seconds flat. It was hours before we were given a
break. When we finally got it, there was one
problem. More than a hundred guys needed to piss
and there were only three port-o-pots. As the
grapevine leaked, there was an option-B. The port-
o-pots formed a privacy barrier. This allowed about
six of us at a time to slip behind and back,
unnoticed, to do our business. It was efficient
and...

"Drill sergeants!"

We scrambled back in line before the drill
sergeants saw, first-hand, what was going on. But
someone obviously snitched!

Called to formation, a big stink was made out of
urinating behind the port-o-pots.

"There's a diseeeeease among us!" said a drill sergeant.

They walked past the ranks, eye-balling us one by one, speaking loudly the whole time about the "disease" and how to keep it from spreading.

"We know who it is. You get one chance to step forward, disease, and the decontamination process can be abbreviated. Otherwise, you'll be quarantined for the remainder of your training."

I wasn't about to step forward. Neither was anybody else. Hell, there were probably two dozen of us at fault, but they just wanted to make an example of one. The only question was who would be the sacrificial lamb. Perhaps the drill sergeants only had one name to work off of – no doubt from whoever snitched.

In my head, I kept rattling off, "Please don't be me – please don't be me – please don't be me."

One of the drill sergeants said, "You had your chance," and walked directly at me.

I knew I was screwed.

"Serrano!"

I almost peed my pants and stepped forward but just when I was about to move, I realized that wasn't my name. It was one of my closest friends.

The public humiliation he withstood was relentless. I felt relieved and guilty just the same.

His bunk in the barracks was separated from the rest of us, taped off in the open bay. He marched separate from us. He ate alone. He showered after everyone else. He was forbidden to look at another human being let alone speak out loud. He was outcast but present.

Two weeks later it was just cruel.

He was going to crack. I could see it in his face, his walk, his everything. I felt so bad for him. It could have been any one of us. As time dragged on, we counted our blessings it wasn't any of us though.

In the mess hall, I was in line with a couple of close friends. I suggested we sit with Serrano. There were no takers. Hell, they blasted that idea from the start. Stationed for basic training on Tank Hill in summer at Fort Jackson was already considered the equivalent of drawing the short straw in the Army. Nobody wanted to make a bad situation any worse. But I couldn't let this ride. Not anymore.

We sat down and I made one last plea for a group effort to come to the aid of our friend. They wouldn't even look me in the eyes. So, I got up, alone, and walked over to Serrano. He was so closed off to the world, mentally, he never saw me coming.

I plopped down across from him and said, "The Yankees suck."

He looked up and for the first time in weeks, his face turned flush with life.

A huge smile spread across his mug and he deadpanned back, "Fuck you, Satullo!"

That's when my head drill sergeant towered above me, "You're going to catch the disease if you don't move!"

I could tell in his eyes that he respected my effort. I could also tell he was not going to reward it. In fact, he was giving me one chance and one chance only to undo what I just did. Strong as I wanted to be, I didn't know if I had the strength to go through what Serrano was going through.

I looked at my friend. He gave me a quick wink. This told me I gave him all he needed to get through from here. I got up, returned to my other friends and the small, cramped mess hall filled back up with the usual noise.

Serrano was cured and rejoined our ranks with a clean bill of health just a couple days later.

The AIDS Pig

AIT in the Army means Advanced Individual Training. It's where you learn your MOS (Military Occupational Specialty). For this, I was stationed at Fort Gordon, Georgia.

Right away, the contrast from basic training was extreme. Here, we could do anything we wanted in evenings and weekends. During the week, we went to school. It was easy compared to what I had been through. The only exception was periodic guard duty. Several of us were selected and taken across base to a large parking lot and barracks. We stood in formation for an inspection along with others from units across the base. Afterward, we entered the barracks where we'd spend the night on and off. In two hour shifts, we were taken to different parts of the base to stand guard. Some beats were done solo and some with a partner. When the shift was over, we had a two hour break back at the barracks before going out again.

It was a crisp fall night. My first assignment was a filling station. I guarded the pumps and the cars out back needing repair. Right away, I noticed I forgot my lighter. I spent my first thirty minutes breaking into a car so I could use the car lighter.

My second time out was with a partner. We had to guard a medical clinic and research center. When we got dropped off, we were briefed and then relieved the previous two guards. When we circled around back, we walked along a fence and what looked like a muddy pit as far as I could see with my flashlight.

"What the hell is this?" I asked.

"This is where they keep the AIDS pig," my partner responded. "You don't know about the AIDS pig?"

I was new so he explained how they had it for research purposes. They actually, intentionally, infected the pig with HIV (Human Immunodeficiency Virus) to study it. This was back when AIDS (Acquired Immune Deficiency Syndrome) was a fairly new scare and to young guys like us, we had no idea how it could or couldn't be spread.

My partner grabbed a thick long branch and reached through the fence to poke at the pig. Eventually, the pig grunted and found the end of the stick; he slobbered and chewed on it. Suddenly, just as I suspected and feared, my partner turned on me and the chase began. He was waiving that stick, running after me, taunting me.

I shouted things over my shoulder like, "This shit aint cool ass-hole!"

He didn't listen.

Eventually, he pitched the stick, laughed at me and we went on with our checks.

I only had guard duty one other time in AIT. The whole scenario played out like the first time around.

When I was doing rounds with another guy out at the clinic, he pointed his flashlight and asked, "What the hell is that?"

"That's the AIDS pig," I said.

It was his first time there, so I explained the story while I fetched a branch thick and long enough to reach through the fence and poke at the pig. Once the pig slobbered it up real nice, I turned to find my partner already backpedaling.

"Stop it. This shit ain't funny," he said to my amusement.

I didn't listen.

Eventually, he fell to the ground and I stood over him with the stick. When I pitched it to the side at the last second, laughing, he got up, lunged into me and we rolled around for a while, wrestling and jabbing each other in a playful manner – not looking to hurt each other.

What better way to pass time on guard duty?

Tattoo

My dad and his brothers grew up on tough streets giving each other tattoos. All they needed was a needle and India ink.

Today, tattoo parlors are everywhere to meet the demand of a culture that is all inked up.

When I was just out of basic training, it was still somewhat of a novelty. Call it a rite of passage but if you served, you got a tat! We weren't going to go the do-it-yourself route so we headed into the city to go to the tat shop that was handed down to us by word of mouth.

I wish I could blame things on a bottle of whiskey and the usual story but we had no excuse. Besides, had we been drinking, the tattoo artist wouldn't have done the job – something about the blood being too thin to scab right.

We browsed through books and wall photos, looking for the right art at the right price. I only had 45 bucks so my pickings were slim. Guys tend to get crosses, chains, fire, or anything that screams don't mess with me, I'm a tough guy. That wasn't my style. Other guys got stuff like the Tasmanian Devil from Bugs Bunny cartoons – still not my style.

I thought long and hard, picturing my arm twenty years down the road. Could I live with this? I sat down convinced.

"Maybe I'll switch to a clean needle," the man said.

I was pretty sure he was opening with a joke he told every newcomer but I wasn't certain.

Afterwards, our shiny, colorful scabs were something to be proud of. We were men.

Many years later, I was splashing my little kids at the pool. It was an affluent community. There were other parents with little ones all around us. I had had my tattoo for so long, I thought as little of it as I do a mole.

That was until my daughter yelled, "Dad, your mouse is wet."

All eyes followed her index finger to my bicep sporting a mouse.

"Why are there bubbles all around his head?" my son asked. "And what is he drinking?"

Top Secret

While I was learning to be a rat rig radio operator in Georgia, my platoon sergeant informed me and another guy I knew that the CID wanted to talk to us.

CID stands for Criminal Investigative Department in the military. We wondered if it had anything to do with our weekend hotel parties. It didn't. We were selected as candidates to move beyond the training for our primary MOS to become satellite communication specialists. We already had secret designations but this job meant we needed a Top Secret security clearance.

As we waited with a few others in a holding room, buzz began. Some relayed rumors about the questioning they had been told to expect. It was stuff like if you ever smoked pot and that sort of thing.

My friend asked what I was going to say and I said, "No."

He asked if that was the truth and I said, "Of course," and smiled.

He said, "Same here."

Well, when it was my turn to go into one of the small rooms to be interrogated by a CID agent, it started very conversationally. Once I was comfortable, he upped the heat quickly. I just answered question after question noticing some repetition. When he asked about drugs of all sorts, I just said no. He fixated on marijuana and wouldn't accept my answer.

He stood up and leaned over the table and looked me square in the eyes and said, "You mean to tell me you never even tried it, not at a high school football game, party, anywhere?"

"No sir."

This went on for 15 or 20 minutes – just this question. I locked in and was not about to change my answer no matter how bad he tried. He was visibly upset with me. He read me the riot act and emphasized the penalty for lying to him. It was clear I'd be tarred and feathered and wished I was dead.

Later, I ran into my friend and asked him how it went. He said that they broke him and he admitted to smoking pot once. But once he cracked, they forced open the flood gates and by the time they were done with him, he admitted to smoking pot something like 17 times. I couldn't help but laugh my ass off. He laughed too, albeit uneasily.

Together, we went to satellite school and then our separate ways.

En route across Germany I was traded from one official to another and found myself at a base where everyone had been deployed to the field except for a couple of non-commissioned officers.

"Wow, we can use one of these," I overheard one say to the other.

The place was like a ghost town so I could hear them in the other room. They were "doctoring" my orders to keep me there. When my next ride strolled in they played dumb but he would have none of it. When he caught them in their lies, he was pissed but forgiving. Everything was changed back and I left with him. That place just gave me a very bad vibe and I was happy I'd never see it again. I cringed at the thought of spending the next few years there. It was so isolated.

When I arrived at my permanent post in Germany, I instantly felt at home because it was a larger base and had signs of life. I was to conduct satellite communication for short range nuclear missiles even though I was still not approved for my Top Secret clearance. It took longer than anyone else I knew. During that time, the CID took my initial 10 references and actually visited my hometown and interviewed each, getting more references from them. I did the math and honestly didn't think I even knew that many people. It must have been a big deal for many because when I'd come home on leave – or even years after the Army – parents of friends, and people I'd barely know, would tell me about the time these guys from the military came asking about me.

Our job was unique in that we could actually refuse an order from an officer under specific circumstances. It was an enlisted man's dream. I wondered if it was more a fantasy. Then, one time while in the field, that specific circumstance presented itself. I was only a PFC (Private First Class) at the time and my superior on duty that night was just a Specialist. Our encrypted messages had a classifications system for importance. One classification was only to be used in true wartime. During a simulated exercise in which missiles were actually erected, one of the lieutenants wanted it to be as real as possible.

Communicating with another base, the lieutenant said to assign it as a "flash" message. I was startled by the request because she should have known better. I nervously explained what that meant and that I couldn't do it.

She didn't like the "backtalk" and said, "It's an order."

I repeated, uncomfortable and worried in this precarious situation, that I could not do it.

She was angry at my refusal, but I knew I'd be in a heap of trouble if I carried out her order. She shouted at my superior. He was sleeping just a few feet away on the floor. During the night, we'd take shifts at the controls. She told him to get up and carry out the order.

He rubbed his eyes, processed in his mind what she was saying to do and then flat out said no as well. He kindly explained as I did but she was hell bent on doing this her way.

Another low ranking officer was brought in and he threatened both of us with punishments if we did not obey his order.

The situation escalated one more level and that's when higher brass put the lieutenants in their place. I managed to conceal my smile at the same time worrying about repercussions down the line.

The ranking officer sternly stated to the lieutenants, "Next time, know this when you want to play general, know that those boys carry live ammunition for a reason – this is not a game!"

The Human Chain

We were teenagers serving on a NATO base in Germany. We often walked several miles from base to a small town. It had a great place to eat, another to party and the only video store around. We used a shortcut that didn't connect to the road leading to base. It followed a pathway behind the British housing outside of the main gate. The path led to a narrow, rural road squeezed between crops.

One evening, we were on the back road and saw a group of British chicks in the distance behind us. A slight hill gave us the cover we needed to disappear from their sight, if they even seen us at all. Slipping into a chest-high corn field, we lay low and waited for our prey. We aimed to scare them, expecting they'd scream and run. We had trouble concealing our unmanly giggles just thinking of how hard we'd soon be laughing when they ran away, scared.

The girls were in their late teens, pretty, bubbly and ripe for our practical joke. They neared, chatting, walking and having fun.

Showtime!

One of us made a deliberate, low, hoarse cough trying to sound as if blood was gurgling out.

Nothing.

We grimaced at one another and gave the nod.

Out came another gurgling, "H-e-l-p ...m-eeee."

One girl stopped and looked into the field, "What was that?"

"I heard it too," another validated.

They all stood there, motionless. We froze, too, but with ear-to-ear grins, proud of our

154

achievement. It was working and any second, they'd run away screaming and we'd roll on the ground laughing.

After a moment, they started to say something amongst themselves.

So again, we brazenly threw out another, "Please, he-lp," followed by faint choking noises.

Our hearts skipped.

Instead of running away, they left the road, arms outstretched at their sides, clasping hands and methodically combing through the short corn like a human chain.

That was not the plan!

"Retreat," we whispered to each other.

We put our low-crawling skills into action and quietly wormed our way deeper into the field, and angling away from the path of the girls.

Proud of our stealth success, we paused to direct another, "H-e-l-p …m-eeee," in their direction.

"I heard it, it's coming from over there," said more than one of the girls.

They turned the human chain toward us again and dragged through the short corn stalks, head and shoulders above.

The hunters were now the prey.

Dusk grew darker and low and behold, a flashlight beamed. Our adrenaline kicked in, the cat-and-mouse game proving more fun than we imagined. How far will these Brits be willing to go?

We went through a third cycle of "help" and retreated again.

We were in so deep, in more ways than one, there was no turning back.

Which way was back?

There was no longer any flashlight to be seen. We became concerned. Someone suggested we keep going deeper figuring we'd plow through to the other side of the field where it may eventually hit the main road to base.

What nobody wanted to admit was we were lost and the girls were gone.

"HELP US!"

Hit Man on the Island

I befriended a tour guide on the ferry from the Italian mainland to Capri. The conversation was fluid despite the teenagers taking turns to beg for smokes once Nicolo lit up. He seemed used to it. Every handout was done non-verbally on his part and with hardly a conscious effort.

The boys were milking it. Once the first kid returned to his friends, smiling, inhaling the carcinogens like he owned the boat, chattering away in Italian, another boy came forward. This cycle played out three times.

Then, without warning, the gravy train stopped.

Nicolo made eye contact with the boys for the first time. He didn't look at the kid standing before him. Rather, he looked through him at the others. He merely shook his head, deliberately, to the left and then back, once. With that, the boys disappeared into the crowd. Nicolo never broke sentence, speaking to me the whole time.

Upon landing at port in the harbor, our tour group sifted through the sea of people and boarded an awaiting bus. It was small, windows open, sending a much welcome breeze through my hair as we shimmied uphill to a villa and stopped.

Whap!

The bus driver and Nicolo babbled away in Italian then we sped off. And I mean we sped with reckless abandon all the way to the next villa. Although it was hot outside, Nicolo seemed to be sweating a lot more than just a moment ago. The fella he smacked with the opening bus door was hottest of all. He, no doubt, was shouting obscenities and threats as we sped away.

Leaning out my open window for fresh air, I saw what happened. I didn't understand the fear induced panic that ensued. A group of several well-dressed middle-aged men were chatting curbside when we rolled up. Nicolo, meanwhile, was chatting to us over a microphone system. Funny, after the door smacked one of the fellas at the curb, Nicolo's voice amplified even louder without the microphone.

Throughout the day, some on the tour periodically asked Nicolo about the incident. Each time he shrugged it off by giving non-answers if he didn't outright ignore the person asking. The tour continued without interruption.

It was dark when we settled on the last ferry leaving the island. Tired, we sat in silence, mostly. A new group of boys scored a few smokes off of Nicolo before being cut off with that half shake of his head.

Then I half-laughed, asking, "Is it often you hit pedestrians with bus doors?"

"It's the first time I hit Mafioso."

157

CHAPTER 4:
GROWING UP BUT WITH
RELAPSES OF IMMATURITY

Wrestling a Bear

We were minding our own business in a back room of a bar, shooting pool. It was on the western edge of Avon Lake. We were celebrating Steve's 21st birthday. Both of us were fresh out of the Army and our other best friend, Mike, was home from college.

A stranger walked in and casually asked if we wanted to wrestle a bear. No's quickly turned to contemplation quickly turned to hell yah, as long as we're all in.

We were led to the parking lot to sign our "rights" away on some forms. Years later, the same owner of Caesar the Wrestling Bear would be in the news for one of his bears mauling a man to death. It doesn't take much imagination to understand how a captive bear trained to bar fight night after night would turn. On this night, we were wrapped in a cocktail of invincibility that combined bravado with ignorance.

We needed to capture this life experience, or death, for the record so we called – of all people – my mom. She agreed to drive across town, bringing her camera. Later, we'd get grainy copies of a video tape shot by a neighbor's friend who was there that night. The neighbor thought he was just watching a bunch of crazies on film until he recognized me, so he dubbed a copy of the tape to give to us.

Caesar was a full grown black bear. He looked enormous, especially when he stood. Plus, he had his teeth and his mouth was not taped closed as some anticipated. He also had massive bear paws and claws that were not restricted at all. The smell of real danger began to seep in as we were introduced to Caesar and given some pointers. Sudden movements, loud noise and over aggressiveness by any of us could make the bear "defensive" and not "playful."

Oh, and one particular pointer stuck with me, "Just make sure he doesn't accidentally hook you in the corner of the mouth with a claw because he'll rip your cheek straight up without knowing it."

The handler sized us up and looked at Mike, Steve and me saying, "Usually, smaller people have a better chance of pinning him down because he is more playful with them."

The reward for doing so was something like a cool grand – certainly incentive to give it our best shot. The pecking order went Mike, Steve then me.

Mike was a tall guy with a pretty solid build. He entered the closed off mat (a.k.a. dance floor) and definitely had a serious look on his face. The bear must have gotten a bad vibe from Mike because he got rather aggressive. The trainer separated the bear from Mike and gave Caesar a firm reprimand. Meanwhile, Mike looked at us as if to say, I want out. But he was in – up to his neck in. The match continued. Mike tried hard, maybe too hard, and the bear got all crazy again – even rearing up on his hind legs. They ended the match and took the bear out to the parking lot to calm him down.

I was so happy Steve was next and not me. When that thing came rumbling back in, it was ready for business. Steve's a scrappy fighter and wasn't fazed by much in those days, but he quickly hit the mat, hard, and looked up …fazed and then some. You could tell there was nothing to be done once that bear had you. Its weight and strength determined your range of movement. It wasn't up to you what happened in there, it was entirely up to Caesar. Moving Caesar would be like trying to move a brick house. It wasn't going to happen unless he allowed it to happen. He wasn't allowing Steve to do much. When Steve came off the floor, he was dripping in sweat, exhausted by the energy he expended.

My turn came. I had tried to learn from observing Mike and Steve plus remembering the pointers the trainer gave us.

Once in the ring with this beast, a voice popped in my head screaming, "What the hell are you doing here?"

I wasn't fairing much better than Steve and Mike. The bear used one paw and swatted me down like a rag doll. Before I knew it, he was on top of me and I couldn't budge. It took every bit of strength I could muster just to move my hand an inch, even then I could only manage to do so because Caesar allowed it to happen. I talked with a friendly, playful and calming voice. I moved slowly and didn't look him in the eyes.

That's when the unthinkable happened. We were both on our feet. I moved in and he went down – because he was playing and took himself down. In an instant, I was on top of this massive creature.

Now, let me slow this description down and zoom in. I went from not knowing what happened to staring at powerful jaws inches from my face, breathing in the animal's hot, stale breath. I slid one hand over and Caesar let me press his paw to the mat. To get the other paw stretched out and down meant I'd basically have to get close enough to kiss Caesar on the mouth, my neck fully exposed.

"A-A-A-A-And we have a ..." before the DJ could say "winner" Caesar was up and I was down.

And that's where I stayed for the rest of my time.

When I regrouped with my friends, none of us felt well. The acid in our stomachs, the exertion out on the floor and the rancid bear smell all over us was all we could stand. We went behind the building, saturated in sweat, and heaved everything from our stomachs and then some.

When I looked up, one of my friends said, "Dude, your neck is bleeding."

Crazy was in the Air

Steve, Eddie and I drove out to visit a summer friend who was at his parents' weekend place.

Summer friend is a term we created to refer to someone we hung out a lot with over one summer but not really before or after.

He took us up by the yacht club and marina along the river feeding into Lake Erie. We hopped a fence and climbed a train trestle.

"We do this all the time," our summer friend said.

And he walked out, following the train tracks, high over the river.

"Don't look down and you'll be all right," he mused.

The thing was you had to look down to know where to place your next step. We had grown up jumping off a cliff into the lake at the edge of our neighborhood but this was different.

"This is crazy!" one of us muttered.

We each said something to that effect as we found ourselves looking at nothing but sky on both sides of us and water below, "This is nuts!"

As we stood cautiously in the breeze, we realized how far up we were. It was hard to imagine actually jumping. Land wrong and then what? Hit a boat and you know what!

"What's that sound?" Steve asked.

"A train but don't worry, we have plenty of time," our friend replied matter of fact.

We didn't know where the sound was coming from and we certainly weren't sticking around to find out.

We looked at each other and said, "Screw this."

But as we turned to walk back, our friend said there wouldn't be enough time. He then went into a spiel that sounded like a safety course on how not to kill ourselves. We listened to him, the train, him. Basically, the gist was to look both ways before jumping to make sure your body wouldn't meet with a passing boat upon landing.

"Feel the tracks!" Eddie said.

And with that, he was the first to take a leap of faith.

Before we saw how his landing went, we looked back and then forward, saw a couple of boats and jumped anyway.

I don't know what went through those boaters' minds when out of nowhere four human cannon balls plunged into the water all around. But by more than one account, they damn near jumped out of their skin judging by the expressions on their faces. One boater looked like he was being electrocuted the way his shocked body gyrated after Steve came within feet of blasting a hole through his boat.

We ignored the angry calls thrown our way by the boaters. Slowly we swam to shore. It was an exhilarating moment for us. But nobody was up for doing it again.

Car Accident

It was summer and we were picking up snowmobiles.

There were five of us crammed into an old Ford Pinto. This was a small car that was once recalled for a faulty gas tank that was rumored to cause fires or explosions upon impact.

I was around 21-years-old. Eddie was a lifelong friend and his mom's boyfriend, Lloyd, needed help. So it was the three of us, our friend Steve and a friend of Lloyd's. The car was well maintained except the seatbelts had been cut out of it. It was Lloyd's pride and joy since he was a teenager, or so Eddie told us.

The three of us friends were in the backseat and Lloyd and his friend were up front. We were cruising down Walker Road towing a trailer. With no warning whatsoever, a lady with a baby sailed through the intersection from our left side, on Jaycox Road, and both cars hit doing 35-40 miles per hour. The only skid marks were those left from tires AFTER the collision.

I was sitting behind the driver and on the side hit. Upon impact, my head careened into the metal divider between the front and backseat side windows. It ricocheted to the middle of the car where it met Eddie's head. An instant later, we were stopped and all was silent if even for a split second. I consciously recognized the fact I was alive. So was everyone in our car. I couldn't believe it. The windshield was shattered to a million pieces and the car was mangled.

I wiggled my toes to make sure I wasn't paralyzed. Then I yelled loudly that I wanted out of the car, now—now—now!

Everyone motivated to get out. That's when I noticed Lloyd's jaw just hanging from his face by loose skin. He had broken it on the steering wheel. The steering wheel was broken too so maybe the dashboard snapped the bone, I don't know. His friend was in shock. His face was shattered much like the windshield. It looked like a jig-saw puzzle – a bloody jig-saw puzzle.

Outside of our car, we heard an engine racing in high speed. The car that hit us was raised on a large rock and landscaping set back from the corner. The three of us friends approached it and looked inside. The driver, a young woman, was smashed in the area where the front seat passenger would put their feet. Her whole body was in that small space. She wasn't moving so we thought she was dead for sure. In the backseat was a baby in a car seat. He had a slight scrape above one of his eyes. It was tiny, just like him but it stood out against his soft creamy skin. He giggled up a storm when he saw us peak in at him.

Eddie and Steve had the sense to go around the other side and somehow wiggle into the tilted car and kill the engine. I just made baby faces at the baby trying to keep him happy.

Nearby, residents flocked to the scene and took some of us into their homes to get first-aid while we waited for an ambulance. An old man took me inside a very old stone home. He patched me up enough to release me back to the professionals. Actually, he said I should stay and he'd get them to come here but I insisted I return to the scene and my friends to help.

When I came back outside, flashing lights were everywhere. Lloyd's friend was in shock as they rolled him into an ambulance. Lloyd was screaming for a cigarette before he was taken to the hospital. They learned you don't tell Lloyd no. Someone obliged and placed a lit smoke in his lips. It was quite a sight to see a man with his jaw dangling to the side of his face dragging a cigarette best he could.

After a few puffs, he pitched it and said, "Now you can take me," got in another ambulance and they were off.

Eventually, we all ended up at the same hospital. By the time I made it through the "assembly line" I learned that everyone survived even though some injuries would stay for a while, even long-term.

Lloyd was horribly upset by the whole thing afterward and burdened himself with guilt even though the accident was the other lady's fault. She had not noticed her stop sign and cruised through at about the same speed we were cruising from a 90 degree angle.

166

Knowing what had happened, it's truly amazing life wasn't lost that day. I don't know how my head took the blows it did without something drastically going wrong.

Down the Road

"Pull off here, I have to take care of something," Tommy said.

"Already? We just left!" I complained.

Having officially started our road trip, I just found out my driving partner had to test to get his driver's license back. Between the written exam and driving exam, I asked how he did.

"I think I got a hundred percent this time," he smiled as an officer came out to meet him. "Let me have your keys."

I had a small sports car, Mazda RX 7, and it was packed to the gills.

"What's all this?" the officer asked, somewhat surprised as she opened the passenger door.

"When I blow this popsicle stand, we're down the road – Florida or bust!" Tommy said with his signature grin and enthusiasm.

She shook her head as if to say, *NOW, I've seen it all!*

Winding through the mountains of West Virginia on the Interstate proved difficult. It was dark, the fog was especially thick and Tommy was sleeping. Numerous times, I almost turned into the dividing wall as my mind played tricks on me. My eyes followed the reflecting strips with such monotony they just danced in my head. After a really close call, I woke Tommy so I'd have a co-pilot.

We switched driving duties at every fill up. The gas tank was nearly empty and we hadn't seen signs for a gas station in a quarter tank or so. We were desperate so we decided that the next time we saw a sign, we'd follow it no matter where it took us, as long as it eventually led us to gasoline.

We ended up miles from the highway, navigating the hilly terrain deep into no-man's land until we finally spotted a glow on the edge of the rural road. It was a run-down place with nothing – and I mean nothing – else around. We pulled in, pumped the gas and went inside, together, to add munchies to our purchase. It was very late at night. So we were surprised to see several guys hanging out.

As we walked past two of them sitting on top of a floor cooler, I noticed their filthy bare feet. Nobody said anything to us except the guy behind the counter and even that exchange was minimal. When he spoke, his accent was so thick, I really couldn't understand him. We could feel all eyes on us, perhaps even some whispering. It was uncomfortable to say the least. And it became obvious to me how easily we could disappear and nobody would ever know what became of us.

When we plopped back into our car seats, Tommy said, "Get the hell out of here!"

I didn't notice until later that I drove two consecutive shifts. It may have been an honest mistake but my co-pilot's nickname was "The Shark!"

Somewhere in Florida, Tommy woke me up. I squinted, the sun was so bright. He pointed my attention to the car keeping pace next to us on the highway. I quickly ran my fingers through my hair, trying to get rid of my "window head." I even had some drool. And that was before we got a Spring Break "peep-show" from the car full of girls pacing us.

About an hour later, we were still full of energy, traveling at our cruising speed of 80MPH. A police car flew up on us like we were in a school zone. Tommy pulled to the slow lane thinking we were busted but the cop car blasted past us, trailed by several other cop cars.

"What the hell, Tom!" I yelled in dismay.

Tommy was in hot pursuit of the police convoy, traveling in excess of 100MPH.

"Oh, they've got bigger fish to fry so I'm taking advantage of our police escort," Tommy said with a grin.

Soon, we found out why. It was a horrific sight. A van of spring breakers must have lost control and rolled for nearly a quarter mile, based on the carnage strewn along side of the highway. We slowed down considerably after that.

We stayed with one of my old Army buddies on the Atlantic coast and hit the beach. One day, we drove to Ft. Lauderdale but spent most of the day at an outdoor bar with a roof. It was raining steadily. That didn't dampen our time. At least that's what I gathered from the other partiers pointing video cameras our way – until "naked man" on a balcony across the street stole the show.

Before scooting up the coast to Daytona, Tommy spent an evening "working" for a friend of my Army buddy. The friend repossessed cars and

Tommy was invited to help him. Tommy had the time of his life.

We rolled into Daytona wondering if we had enough money left for a room and if any rooms were even available. If not, we decided we could just live out of the car for a few days. A hotel on the beach advertised Playboy Bunnies and MTV as their guests. We were amazed that a room had recently become available. We snatched it, no questions asked.

I'm not sure about the statute of limitations so I'll skip some of the other shenanigans we got into but worth a mention was the start of our last night. We left the outside concert at our hotel and retreated to an indoor club. Sitting at a long bar, we were an island unto ourselves. Partying was going on all around but not where we perched. Our little pocket of paradise disappeared quickly when a bunch of guys surrounded us. They seemed intent on squeezing us out to claim the bar as their own.

Tommy nodded my attention toward one of the guys and said in a star-struck voice, "I think that's Tone Loc!"

"Who?"

"You know, the guy that sings, Wild Thing," Tommy explained. "This must be his entourage."

I clanked my beer glass against Tom's and loudly broke into song, "WILD THING! YOU MAKE MY HEART SING. YOU MAKE EVERYTHING ..."

Tommy tried to shut me up, insisting I was singing the wrong "Wild Thing," but the entourage finished, "...GROOVY."

The Little Brick Shop

At the corner of our neighborhood, growing up, there were a couple of buildings that had stores such as Stop -N- Go, Lawson's and Convenient over the years. When we were kids, it was where we used to get ice cream, pop and candy. Our favorite place was just a few doors down, set back beside an auto repair shop. It was a little brick shop. An older lady owned it. We called her Mrs. D.

The place was largely a beer store. It even had a makeshift bar in back where there always seemed to be one man on a stool, midday, watching an old television. Up front was a counter; in front of it was a cooler with freezer pops and behind it was candy land. Oh, and baseball cards. Mrs. D always smiled when we came in with our loose change or returnable bottles that we found along roadsides. We exchanged these for freezer pops, usually, or bottles of pop, candy bars and packs of baseball cards.

On the far side of the counter was a wall of candy held up high on metal racks. Beyond that were heavy brown cardboard boxes of beer stacked anywhere from one to seven high and two or three deep. We'd perch up there in our box thrones and talk, laugh, eat and open baseball cards until Mrs. D would finally peek through some candy boxes and say we had to move along. She usually gave us a good half-hour.

Running around all day, as boys, we'd find the need to pee, especially after drinking pop. There was usually no place near to go so we'd walk along the side wall of the little brick shop, far enough to get out of sight and "go" on the wall. Sometimes, we'd use our stream to graffiti words, then laugh and run away down a path that led out onto another street.

I'm not sure when the shop finally closed. I was older and didn't go there anymore. When I got out of the Army and picked up some classes at the community college, waiting to move and transfer to a university the following fall, I got a side job making and delivering pizzas. The pizza shop was inside what used to be Mrs. D's little brick shop. The interior was completely different. The pizza place was owned by a nice old man and his wife – a spirited Italian woman. Mr. and Mrs. C had shops at both ends of town. I made pizza at the far one and delivered pizzas from the little brick shop at the edge of my neighborhood.

Inside, there were booths where we used to sit on boxes while eating candy as kids. It was a slow midweek night and we didn't need one delivery driver, let alone two. It was very untypical. So, my friend, Eddie (the other driver), and I just sat and talked in one of the booths. Mr. C slipped in and small talked along with us. Something piqued our interest about Mr. C so we asked questions about his life. He really piqued our interest when he told us what it was like to storm northern European beaches and then march through Europe during World War II. Now to us, this was just sweet old man C. But the stories he told of that invasion made our hair stand on end. Eddie's cigarette turned into one long ash still in the shape of a cigarette. His hand never moved and he never took his eyes off the old man.

When Mr. C described the liberation of concentration camps, we hung on his every word. Empathy filled us. The night was still and the lighting dim. His voice reached into our hearts and gave a mighty pull. We could have listened to him until closing and beyond.

"Get up and get in the kitchen, these pizzas aren't going to make themselves," Mrs. C appeared in an apron. "Besides, do you think these boys really want to hear your tired old stories all night?"

Avon Lake's Finest

As a kid growing up in a small town, I experienced more than my share of mischief. But I had great respect for the men in blue.

Officers were friendly and some even had a great sense of humor. I should know; I seemed to run into them here and there over the years. One or two had a chip on their shoulder and of course, anyone could have a bad day. Some serious crimes happened from time to time but mostly the police kept us kids in check. That isn't to say there weren't kids doing some awful things, such as a druggie holding up old man Kekic's gas station with a knife.

Old man Kekic had a small gas station in front of his house on Lake Road. When Mom pulled in, he'd pump the gas, check the oil, wash the windshield, and even check the tire pressure. Mom usually went inside to look at the tubs of candy to get us a surprise.

When old man Kekic had little kids alone, he'd stick his head in the window and ask in a gruff voice and menacing face, "Who did it?"

We'd all squeeze to the far corner of the backseat.

"When I find out, I'm goin' ta THROW ya in the lake!"

Then he'd pull out of the window and finish servicing the car. It was his way of teasing us little kids I suppose, but he carried the shtick a little too well. It wasn't until we were older and used to take a back trail to the station for candy runs that we began to see him for the lovable old man he was.

Anyway, one of my best friend's dad was on the police force. He was what we considered a cool cop. If you got stuck doing doughnuts with a car in a snowy parking lot before school, he didn't ask how you got in the predicament, he'd help you get out.

When I was a summer camp counselor for little kids in town, I asked my friend's dad to talk to them about summer safety. I'll always remember him saying it was something he didn't like to do but it had to be done. I didn't understand at first. Then he explained that seeing the innocence of youth replaced with the realization of the bad things that could happen in life was a message he did not like delivering.

We loved most of the police officers, even those of us who saw them a little more than we liked in the course of our youth. But I'll never forget the day I came to consciously respect those who had the job of serving and protecting. I was making pizzas across town and just finished my last batch. It was a particularly busy day and the delivery driver

174

was humping it for hours. I told him I'd make the next run so he could eat. He smiled and said thanks.

On my drive back to the shop, I noticed a crowd gathering right in front of the police station. In small towns like ours you couldn't resist seeing what all the fuss was about. So I pulled into a lot, walked up to the station and peered through the crowd. A car had hit a huge tree out front and a rather large man was lying in the grass. One of the younger officers was pumping the man's chest and doing all he could to revive him. Some little kids were crying. Adults attempted to shield them from the scene. A stranger next to me whispered that he thought that the kids had also been in the accident.

Everyone watched in silence, pretty much, as the officer tried to revive the man. I felt for the officer. I pleaded silently for the man to come back to life but he was dead. The officer kept trying. This went on so long it was clear there wasn't going to be a miracle. The officer, exhausted, wouldn't stop. My heart broke.

On the way back to the pizza shop, my eyes welled up at the tragedy I just witnessed. I realized how often our police officers, firefighters and paramedics experienced horrific accidents. I understood that one of the reasons Avon Lake was such a beautiful community to raise a family was because of men and women like these, serving in harm's way.

When I returned to the pizza shop, I did what most people would do and said to the girls inside, "You're not going to believe this ..."

175

One put her index finger to her mouth and the other whispered, "We know."

I was confused.

They said that our delivery driver just got a phone call. The man who died was his father.

Jake

My college apartment was missing something. I decided it was a bird.

So, I went to the mall with my new girlfriend, Becky. In the entry to a small pet store was a huge bin with parakeets. Their wings were clipped, so they couldn't fly. But they could run – from one side of the open bin to the other. We went one way and they went the other. It was funny to see a stampede of tiny colorful birds bee-bopping in a rush.

Then we noticed little ole Jake (a name we'd give him later). He was smaller than the rest of the birds. When they ran, he couldn't keep up so he tripped and got trampled. When we moved to the other side, the birds ran him over again …and again. After torturing the poor thing so we could laugh at his misfortune, we did the humane thing and saved him.

Jake was like another roommate. With his cage door open, he was free to come and go as he pleased. His freedom grew along with his wings. Soon, he learned his name and about five different whistles. I didn't whistle but my roommate did. Jake understood my verbal commands.

"Come here, Jake."

He'd flutter across the room and land on my shoulder. He often perched on our shoulders or heads. It was fun to watch him plop around the couch while we watched TV or wander around the kitchen when we'd cook. And by cook I mean throw something in the microwave for 3 minutes. Sometimes we couldn't tell if our food was done because Jake learned to imitate the microwave beep.

This bird was special. We could swear he had personality, even a sense of humor. He was the cat's meow. Okay, bad reference.

After exams, I conked out on the couch. It was a deep sleep. It morphed into a nightmare. I couldn't breathe. I was suffocating. Startled, I opened my eyes. That's when the horror really began. On my chin was little Jake. His beak was deep up one of my nostrils mining for gold nuggets. I was horrified because he was really going to town, frantically wiggling around way inside there and then quickly shifting to the opposite nostril to do the same. As I regained consciousness, my reaction was delayed. For a brief moment, I'll admit, it tickled so good. Then, I freaked out and swatted him. I damn near killed the little bugger.

When it came time for Christmas break, I had to pack my car with all my clothes so I could use Mom and Dad's washer when I got home. This meant multiple trips to and from my car. It was very cold outside so I figured it would be best to move Jake last. I used the sliding glass doors because it was closest to the parking lot. Each time, I took note of Jake across the room on top of his cage. It was far enough to quickly slide the door open, bend down and put a basket or box on the patio, and close the door behind me.

On my third trip, I looked at Jake, opened the door, bent down and heard a brief flutter over my head.

I never saw him again.

Ask-A-Nurse

I had a reoccurring sharp pain in my chest. It made me afraid to breathe deep. I knew it was anxiety but my girlfriend, Becky, and her roommates had other ideas.

"You should call the number for Ask-A-Nurse," suggested one.

This was a new telephone service offered by the hospital. You could call, describe your symptoms, and a nurse would tell you how to proceed.

The pressure built and I'm not talking about my chest. I reluctantly called the phone number.

"You need to go to the emergency room, now," said the nurse over the phone.

I expected as much. Now my anxiety was heightened, so I let Becky take me to the hospital.

The emergency personnel put me in a private room and then proceeded to stick me all over and then hook me up to a machine. Becky stayed by my side holding my hand, eyes glued to the monitor that was recording my pulsating heart.

"Was that it? Did you feel it?" she asked as soon as the line spiked up briefly and went back to normal.

I did feel it but that didn't make me feel any better so it spiked again.

"Did you—"

"STOP THAT!"

Time passed. I was uncomfortable. She was still glued to the monitor. While we were waiting, I had an idea to better entertain ourselves – by that I mean myself. Discreetly slipping an arm out to my side, over the far end of the bed, I shook it rapidly and immediately dropped it back to my side.

"Oh my God! Are you okay?" she yelled while literally jumping into mid-air.

When her feet hit the floor, I was laughing so damn hard I thought everything stuck to me was going to rip right off. In about three seconds, she went from alarm, to anger, to laughing as hard as I was.

The doctor came in with a nurse. They wanted urine. I was instructed to go to the bathroom and return to my room where they would catch up with me later.

I don't know how much they needed but I filled that cup and then some.

Coming back to the room, I shut the door and started making "Jaws music" as I held the cup out in front of me, slowly closing in on Becky. She backed away half-laughing and half-horrified. My attack went on, the threatening cup of urine as my weapon.

Finally, I had her trapped into a corner. She was on her butt, with all four limbs extended out to keep me away. I had the cup held high, taunting her. We were both laughing pretty loudly.

That's when the doctor walked in.

179

Oh, and Becky – she would eventually marry me.

First Impressions

We were getting serious, so much so that it was time for my girlfriend, Becky, to bring me home to her parents. It wasn't just any trip home. It was to go to her cousin's wedding.

The morning of the wedding, Becky's mother entered the kitchen. She is one of the most genuinely kind persons I had ever met. She passed quickly, dropping some stern words my way. It was like a hit and run and I didn't get the license plate. Maybe it was the accent. I asked Becky what just happened.

"You left the seat up …and she fell in."

So I was off to a good start.

We were in college and I was still a smoker. Becky despised it and forbade me to light up around her. At the wedding reception the craving became too much. I slipped into the men's room and lit up over the sink. I dragged that stick fast and hard. I felt like a junkie alone in a dirty place getting his fix. The door popped open and as I looked up and blew smoke out, I realized it was Becky's father. He pretended he hadn't seen me as he turned toward the urinal.

I snuffed out the butt and on my way out, I uncomfortably said, "By the way, I smoke."

The brews went down fast and easy after that. Then, I did something completely out of character. I took the 90-year-old granny out on the dance

180

floor. Yep, I was "that guy." The place howled with approval.

There I was, swinging it with granny, hoping she wouldn't break a hip.

I could see arms reaching to tug shoulders in the crowd. Fingers pointed and lips moved, "Who's *that guy?*"

"Becky's boyfriend."

The mother of the groom, Becky's aunt, seemed as spirited as I was, "You two are next – I know. You're made for each other."

One of the uncles was holding court at a nearby table trying to explain his philosophy of the overall party scene to Becky's dad. It was something he called, "The dance of the unborn children."

On the way home, I sat in the backseat staring out the dark window, cringing at the thoughts of the night. The silence was broken by Becky's dad. Out of the corner of my eye, I caught a glimpse of him in the rear view mirror as he was driving.

His eyes looked into that mirror back at me and he mumbled something as if it were meant for my ears only, "Some people may seem great to everyone else but nobody's ever good enough for your daughter."

Practical Joke Gone Bad

Jerry was about as clean cut as they come. It was no wonder that he freaked out one of his new fraternity brothers when they came back to our house after a party. Next door was a cute little home, well-kept for our neighborhood, well-kept

181

for being vacant. And with the lights on timers, you'd never suspect that no one lived there.

Before Evan could even ask what Jerry was doing, Jerry picked up a rock the size of his head. Who knows what he had in mind, but he insists it was much less crazy than what happened. Once he hoisted the rock over his head, the weight threw him off balance. He staggered into the neighbor's yard – our houses were close – and let go before he hurt himself. The rock smashed through a window.

Jerry sprang to his feet to tell Evan that no one lived there. Evan had already run to his car and peeled out.

The way Jerry told us the story it seemed as if we were listening to a confession. But the sins would only get deeper.

First, we taped a note to the front door of the neighboring house saying we were responsible for the broken window and would be replacing it. Then, a slippery slope of bad decisions ensued.

We loved pulling practical jokes. To really pull off this latest prank, we changed the answering machine message at a girlfriend's house. It took a while but we finally got a complete message recorded without blowing up in laughter.

"Hello, you've reached the desk of Mitchell and Schmidt at station 12. Leave a message." We were careful not to impersonate an officer but were vague enough to let the imagination run wild.

Then, we auditioned for the real zinger. The gig went to our housemate with the deepest voice. He promptly called Evan but his roommate answered, instead.

"I'm sorry, did you say …," the roommate's voice turned very formal and compliant.

"Indeed. We just want to ask Evan a few questions. You see, someone reported a car fleeing the scene of an incident last night, having his license plate number. The incident resulted in an elderly couple suffering injuries from broken glass. They're okay but we'd like to talk to Evan. Have him call us when he returns."

The roommate was loud and clear, "Yes sir! You can count on me."

We hung up and laughed for a while, taking turns saying, "Yes sir! You can count on me."

Eventually, we got bored and hungry so we went out for burgers. The burger-outing turned into a couple of hours shooting pool.

When we returned, we called down to the girlfriend's house to check the answering machine. No new messages. So, we called Evan and got the roommate again.

"Oh, yes sir, I gave him the message as soon as he came in. He tried to call you right away. Then, he left here to drive there and turn himself in."

We hung up. Eyes bulged. Jaws dropped.

Down at the nearest police station, Evan threw himself at the mercy of whoever would listen to him hyperventilate the details. They checked the reports from the night before – twice.

Finally, "Give me your name again son. Full name. Address. Phone. License…If we get a report like this, you'll be the first one we call."

Ding!

Jerry and I were watching TV on an ancient, wooden floor model. The screen went black. The picture tube must be shot, we thought. We called around and determined it wasn't worth a repair. By bedtime, only one housemate didn't know about the loss of our monstrosity of a television.

We figured it was good for one more show – one more prank.

Mark came home from the library. He was the most studious of us all. He had an exam in the morning and thought he was the last one up. The rest of us made ourselves scarce, hoping to get the show on the road.

Lights went out and all was quiet. We heard Mark's bedsprings squeak when he hit the sheets. We were brimming with anticipation. Jerry was taking his good ole time. We began to suspect he chickened out.

Then, there was stirring.

Jerry shouted, "Those damn Cavs!"

He was faking anger at a Cleveland Cavalier's loss.

He cussed some more about the Cavs and said, "I can't take it anymore!"

Pause.

DING!

The plan was for Jerry to smash the TV screen with a baseball bat to get a rise out Mark. The screen obviously had different plans. Nobody realized how thick that sucker was.

Then, another pause.

"Damn Cavs!"

DING!

Nothing.

DING!

Pause.

DING-DING-DING!

I almost suffocated laughing because my head was so far buried beneath a pile of blankets.

"What are you doing!" called out Mark.

Finally, *SMASH!*

It was immediately followed by *CRACK* as Mark's door blasted open and hit the wall. He stormed out, tackled Jerry and wrangled the bat from him. He then proceeded to beat him with his fists.

Jerry pleaded for his life and all we could do to save him was roll out, laughing hysterically.

Bird in the Hand

This story starts on a snowy spring night at our college rental home. Jerry cranked the heat as high as the thermostat would allow and declared it summertime. We packed coolers with snow and beer, set-up lawn chairs and played golf.

Our house was a par-5. We'd tee-off with our putters from my bedroom in the front of the house to get the ball to the living room. Then we had to play the slants in the floors just right to get the ball to roll through the dining room and into the kitchen. If it banked off the sink just right, you'd be sitting pretty at the top of three steps going to the sunken, back family room. That's where the cup was.

With our girlfriends in bikinis and the smell of suntan lotion in the air, college life was never better considering it was too snowy to go anywhere else.

The next day, it was warm outside. The snow melted quickly. We all left for the weekend – thank goodness!

I was the first to return. My girlfriend, Becky, was with me. She noticed something was wrong with our two parakeets. Both were at the bottom of the cage, dying. We took them out and held them, wondering what could be wrong. Becky said to call my dad. Whenever I needed answers, my dad was the go-to guy.

"You have a gas leak. Get out of the house," he said immediately. "Give the birds fresh air and call the gas company."

Becky and I turned off the thermostat, opened windows and we went outside with the birds and cordless phone.

The gas company sent a man within the hour and he said we had major leaks in and outside of the house. The landlord had to be called to approve the emergency repairs. Meanwhile, with the gas off and windows open, it was safe to reenter the house. The birds weren't getting any better. In fact, one died and the other seemed like it was suffering a lot.

I called Dad again.

"Honestly, Rocky, if it's suffering that bad, you might want to consider helping it along."

"What do you mean, Dad?"

He explained that when a pet is suffering, sometimes it's better to take it to the vet to be euthanized. We all knew I wasn't taking the parakeet to the vet so he suggested I fill up the sink, hold it under and it would be for the best.

I got off the phone and urged the bird to get better. It got worse. It was difficult to watch. Then, I urged it to die quickly. It didn't listen. It just made noises and scratched in a circle in the corner of the cage. So, I filled up the sink.

It only took a matter of seconds but every second seemed like a minute to me. The little bird squirmed in my palm. I decided that I couldn't go through with it, but just as I was going to pull it up it gave a hard thrash and was motionless.

Jerry came home during this time. He walked inside the front door, which had a direct line of sight through the front room, dining room and into the kitchen. I had turned to see him walking toward me just as my hand was feeling the thrash of my bird. He knew something was awry. My eyes probably gave it away.

"What are you doing?" he asked, passing by me.

"Drowning a bird."

"Ya, right." He knew that couldn't be true.

I held up the wet, limp bird.

Graffiti

When all of our housemates set out for an afternoon at the local pool hall, two of us had to remain behind to study and complete schoolwork.

When we finally finished, we found ourselves with spare time to just chill out in the living room. We were sipping coffee.

Jerry leaned over, set his mug on a table and said, "I'm curious."

Jerry was destined to become "Mr. Real Estate." He already had a license. He knew a lot about houses and just had a suspicion about this one we were living in. He moved a chair and carefully peeled back the hideous puke green carpet.

"Oh my, check this out," he said.

He pulled the corner of the carpet up so I could appreciate the old wood floor below. It was better looking than many modern wood floors. It still had a shine to it as if the carpeting had preserved it for decades, which was how old the shabby carpeting looked.

"Let's tear this up and show off this wood!" he said, growing excited.

We called the landlord and he actually stopped by to see what we were talking about.

"If you guys do the labor and pull up all the staples and what not, cut, roll and tie the carpet for haul away, you can have at it," he said.

The landlord left and we went to work. But before we tore out the carpet we had other ideas. We grabbed a trash bag full of beer empties from a party we had over the weekend and scattered them everywhere in the living room and dining room. It was one of those older homes where both rooms connected into what was really just one giant spread. Each of our bedrooms connected to these rooms off to the side. Then, we moved the furniture a bit and tossed things around like a real ruckus took place.

We were ready for the masterpiece – the practical joke of the year.

In the garage we found spray paint and house paint, the kind you brush on thick and wide. We came back inside and made a careful mess. We were careful not to ruin the walls or furniture but we went nuts on that old carpeting. We knew we could destroy it but our roommates out drinking had no clue.

So, we tried our hands at graffiti and added a touch of profanity at the end of arrows pointing to different bedroom doors. It was stuff like "Ron gives ..." or "Mark is a ..." or "Tim sucks ..." We didn't hold back. It was bold. It was bad. We laughed hard, trying to out-do one another. We painted awful pictures and sayings in a rainbow of colors splattered EVERYWHERE!

"Here they come!"

We started to fake fight and shouted obscenities at each other. Our three roommates walked in the front door thinking stress got the better of us. They were in a great mood after spending so much time shooting pool. One by one they entered and their jaws hit the floor.

"Whaaaat did youuuu dooooo?" said roomy one.

"Holy crap, we're dead!" said roomy two.

"YOU SUNNAVA BITCHES! YER PAYING FOR THIS," shouted roomy three.

And they sprang across the room and proceeded to kick the shit out of us for real! The problem was we felt no pain we were laughing so damn hard.

Minutes later, we were still trying to force words through our laughter. Eventually, we hit the point that we actually felt the beating and thus did a better job of communicating.

The walloping slowed and our roomies listened, "What?"

Once they realized the hoax, we all collapsed on couches, exhausted, and scanned the masterpiece we had created.

"You sons-a-bitches."

Bounced

The bar was just around the corner from our college home. For a long time, it was our secret watering hole, away from the usual sardine cans. That was before we showed other friends and they showed friends and so on until it was the newest coolest place to hang. And it had a pool table.

We had been going there for so long that Zeke – the owner – knew us pretty well. He was a big man. Zeke asked if I wanted to make some extra money checking IDs on weekends. It sounded good to me.

My first night on the job, it was quiet enough I could shoot pool by the back (main) door. I was a streaky pool player. Some nights I was the cut master and could run a table or close to it. Other nights I couldn't hit the broad side of a barn. I grew up with a pool table and played Dad often so you'd think I'd be more consistent but I wasn't. On this evening, I could do no wrong. And my opponents, part of the new crowd that thought they owned the place, didn't like me taking their money.

The place got crowded fast so I had one eye on the door, having to check IDs, and one eye on the cue ball. I lost my edge and lost the game. Boy did those guys let me know it too. Later in the night,

190

the place was a sardine can and Zeke said not to let anyone else in.

Suddenly, I was a bouncer. I didn't look like a bouncer and surely didn't feel like one. Two guys walked up and I had to hold them back with an extended arm when they didn't think I was serious when I said they couldn't come in until two people left. They were not pleased and they stood there glaring at me. Then, the two guys I was shooting pool with earlier came up and asked what the problem was. All four of these guys pegged me as enemy #1. The two that hated me from shooting pool earlier mouthed off to me. One gave me a tough guy nudge so I slammed him into the pool table. The pool players were upset now too.

Zeke appeared next to me and nobody messed with Zeke. The guy I shoved was long gone. The other guy pleaded his case to Zeke.

Zeke said, "Not inside," and threw me to the wolves.

As anger flooded my veins, I walked out with a head of steam thinking I could take this dude no problem. But there was a problem.

The two guys I wouldn't let in were hanging back in the short hallway between doors out back. I barely paid attention as I whisked by to get outside and take care of business. Hell, I figured people would pour out to watch the fight. Little did I know, Zeke shut the door after my original opponent followed me outside and didn't let anyone else pass.

When I wheeled around, there were three guys in front of me when I expected one. I instantly knew my ass was grass. In the blink of an eye I decided I was only going to get in one punch so I would have to make it a good one. I hit the biggest guy with an uppercut to the chin and then it was lights out …for me.

I had never been beaten so badly and I had never seen anyone beaten so badly. They were relentless. The blows came from all three and from all directions. They hit me with fists, elbows, feet and knees. When the flurry finally ended, I was all the way across a four lane road in a gravel lot, face down in a mud puddle, choking on my own blood-mud-water cocktail. I looked up and the guy who was supposed to be my only opponent was standing over me with a large chunk of broken concrete in his hand, held high over his head.

"Dooon't do thaaat," I forced softly from my lips. It was all I could say.

The only thing between me and my skull being crushed in was my pathetic raised hand and pleading eyes. He dropped the chunk of concrete and walked away.

I struggled to my feet and limp-walked across the street to the edge of the parking lot. At the far end were two of the guys ready to head back into the bar but the one I punched walked "with" me, jawing up a storm.

"Not so tough now. Some bouncer!" He went on and on.

When I saw the other two call out before going through the door, it was a 50-50 decision as to whether or not I should go after this asshole since it would be a one-on-one fight. Adrenaline surged through me. I decided if he didn't hit me, I would keep walking. Once I entered the darkness beyond the parking lot lights, he went his separate way.

I managed to pass my dark house and get halfway down the street to where my girlfriend, Becky, lived. The expressions on her and her roommates' faces scared the hell out of me. One of the roommates' boyfriends was there. They carried me upstairs, filled a tub of water, and set me in it. I had head-to-toe open wounds and gravel embedded way under my skin, everywhere it seemed. I barely remained conscious as they took care of me. I didn't have medical insurance so this treatment was going to have to do. Fortunately, I had no broken bones. It was hard to fathom but I didn't. My overall numbness subsided enough that I could feel my caretakers digging into my scalp, elbows, shoulders and knees to remove fine gravel and dirt. Eventually I was cleaned and patched up, but it took hours. I was embarrassed to have to be cared for like that. On the other hand, I did feel like I was scratching at death's door so I let humility wash over me in waves.

Not long afterward, "recovered," I went with Becky to her extended family Thanksgiving. Her dad's side of the family had yet to meet me. They had heard about me but nobody forewarned them about my "new look." I walked in still sporting black eyes (one was a real nice shiner) and some raw cuts above the neck that weren't yet healed.

My wife's adult cousins, two guys, instantly warmed up to me. The rest, I'm not so sure.

A month later, I asked Becky to marry me.

Extra Extra

We lived off campus at the wrong end of town. You couldn't have a pizza delivered because someone shot a driver.

My roommates weren't home on this night. My bedroom window overlooked the front porch. In the early morning when it was pitch black outside, I awoke to a noise. I lay still and listened for it again. Someone was on the porch.

I shook my fiancé, Becky, awake.

"It sounds like they're trying to get in," she said, sitting up straight.

I grabbed a dusty bowie knife I had stashed just for such an occasion. Damn if they weren't trying to break in. Fear ripped through my body. I ripped up the blinds, streetlight highlighting my shirtless torso.

Brandishing this blade overhead, I shouted, "You better get the %#@*&%! off my porch you %#@*&%^$%!"

Before I could finish, there were two heavy thuds, a quick pitter-patter of feet, car doors slamming and the sound of burning rubber.

We went onto the porch to find stacks and stacks and stacks of the Sunday edition of the Toledo newspaper.

A few hours later, I was sipping coffee, reading one of my hundred or so newspapers when the guy next door walked around his yard, searching for something, with a puzzled look.

"If you're looking for newspapers to deliver, they put 'em on my porch by mistake," I said.

He was relieved.

As we loaded his car, I said, "You might be a little short today."

Dyslexia

I never seemed to grasp speaking in a foreign tongue. I'd spend three times as long as anyone else studying Spanish in college before dropping the course. I also dropped it in high school. Now, I had no choice. My major in college required four quarters of a foreign language class. These weren't three or four credit hour courses, they were five credit hours each, 20 total. My hopes for my grade point average hung in the balance.

Imagine my delight when I learned that the Latin course only required reading and writing, not speaking. That sounded easier. It was a dead language and I was alive with confidence.

During my first quarter I did very well – all things considered. The second quarter, I was very average.

I decided to take the third quarter over summer when the quarter was condensed. Quickly, I fell behind in my studies. After doing poorly on the first exam, I noticed something and put my newly discovered observation to the test. The professor would pick a part of a story for us to translate. It was no small task but I memorized the story word for word. During the test, I merely needed to identify a trigger word or phrase at the beginning and end of the passage he chose to give us for translation. From there, I just wrote from memory.

It worked.

I spent the rest of the quarter getting pretty decent scores. On one paper, a trigger phrase appeared twice so I gave an extra paragraph by accident.

The professor wrote a comment back, "You must have really enjoyed this one to go beyond what the test required."

Whew. I only had one more quarter of Latin to go. But there was one problem. It was like going straight from Latin II to Latin IV.

On the first day of class in my final quarter of college, provided I passed Latin, the teacher said words he'd regret, "As long as you actively participate on a consistent basis in this class, you will get at least a C."

This class met Monday through Friday, one hour per day, five days per week. And day after day, I humiliated myself by raising my hand to volunteer to answer a question. I would ALWAYS get the answer wrong. Sometimes, I could see the facial expressions from students around me wondering what my deal was. It was grueling to voluntarily subject myself to such repeated embarrassment but there was no alternative. I couldn't learn Latin III overnight. This was the only card I had to play and I was playing it to the "T" hoping my professor was good for his word.

He was a young teacher. And he was about to learn a lesson.

After the final exam, I called to ask for a meeting with him. In his office, I reminded him of his promise. Right away he backed away from it. But I persisted. And I persisted. I reminded him of my

DAILY participation, which more than defined consistent.

He was backed into a corner and then he tried for an out that I badly wanted to give him.

"Do you suffer from dyslexia?"

I thought about it for a second that dragged on like a year. I couldn't risk being caught in a lie and jeopardize all that I had worked for. I had to play my cards, not his.

"No."

When I got my report card, I had earned the grade C-minus. Technically, I'm not sure that's a "C" but I wasn't going to look a gift horse in the mouth.

And that's how I got a Bachelor's Degree in Public Relations.

CHAPTER 5:
RESPONSIBLE FAMILY MAN – SORT OF

Blowup Doll

I had been working 70 hours per week for nearly two months straight doing everything possible to make sure our national sales conference went off without a hitch.

We were in Chicago for the conference.

Now, I didn't really know what to do when one of our senior officers asked a favor of me.

"I want to be clear that you don't need to do this for me," he prefaced the request.

Several things went through my mind. I was eager to climb the corporate ladder and wanted to be a team player as long as I wasn't asked to do anything unethical. Was this request unethical? And finally, I asked myself: Why doesn't this wussy just do it himself?

"Ya, no problem, James."

I got directions from the hotel concierge. The store was walking distance. By that I mean within a mile or two from the hotel.

There I was, comparison shopping sex dolls. I found one that was just right for the cash budget James had given me. I paid for it and as luck would have it, they did not have a large enough bag for my purchase. So, I left the store and tried to hail a cab immediately. Again, luck was not with me. I had to hoof it back to the hotel, in a suit, with a blow-up doll's picture sprawled across both sides of the box.

It was broad daylight. At each crosswalk, the double-takes, fast glances, and long stares penetrated my psyche.

Someone had the audacity to call out, loudly, "Gonna get your freak on tonight are ya?"

The humiliation!

Halfway back, I suppressed my embarrassment and decided to have fun with my predicament.

When someone's eyes bulged, I'd look at them and say things like, "She sure got a purdy mouth don't she?"

I never saw people scurry so fast.

When James opened his door, after several knocks, he stood before me in a towel. The irony didn't escape me.

"Here it is," I said handing him the box.

He laughed heartily and said he owed me big-time.

James had lost a mere five dollar bet with a senior officer at a major Chicago financial services company years ago. He had always hounded James to pay up. So, James arranged to have the blowup doll placed in this guy's office chair holding a five dollar bill in her ...hand.

The next night, on a dinner cruise, I finally met the senior management team of this major Chicago financial services company. They all knew me by name even though this was the first time we actually met.

At first they chased me down, laughing and calling me a "Sunnavabitch!"

Then I was made to feel a part of their circle.

Highway to Hell

I spent nearly a decade with some of the most ambitious people I had ever met. It was in the financial services industry. There was a group of us vying to be the next VP in the company before we were 30 years old. You can imagine the personalities.

After a promotion to Marketing Manager, I was rewarded with a road trip to recruit some top-producing, independent financial planners and their organizations. A senior officer drove (I'll call him "boss man") along with us three passengers. At 5:00 a.m., coffee opened our eyes. Not by ingestion mind you but by spilling on two of our laps as boss man whipped around another car, doing 90 MPH on the Ohio Turnpike. The screams were deafening. He laughed when he realized our crotches were scalding hot. He proceeded to tell us a story about opening the passenger window on someone in the middle of a car wash just to enjoy their drenching.

We laughed with the boss man. Then, the early morning yawns returned. That's when boss man crept up on an unsuspecting motorist in the fast lane but not going all that fast. Did I mention the early hour? With a wicked smile, boss man – right on this poor soul's bumper – laid on the horn. There was a delayed reaction by the driver in front of us. He probably froze with shock. Then, he swerved into the other lane so sharply, I thought he was either going off the road or flipping his car. Fortunately, he recovered. Although I don't think any of us did before this day would be through.

By the end of the day, we successfully recruited two sizeable new offices of independent financial planners who agreed to license with us. The boss man suggested drinks before the trip home but there were no takers. We already had doubts about making it home alive.

I wish I could say that meant for a boring return trip but it wasn't.

In a highway traffic jam that slowed us down to about five miles per hour, we found ourselves next to a carful of young women. Boss man put on a friendly conversational voice and actually began chatting with the passengers of this car cruising right next to us.

Then, he deadpanned, "Can I ask a serious question?"

They nodded, yes.

Without hesitation, he raised his butt up and out of the window while he was driving, albeit at a snail's pace, and asked, "I have an exercise tape called Buns of Steel, tell me, is it working?"

I think we all, in both cars, died right there.

As the day darkened, we all grew silent, traveling steady at about 80 MPH. Then, boss man tapped the two of us riding in the back seat. Once he knew he got our attention, he put his index finger to his lips and then gestured at the guy sleeping in the passenger seat.

My heart lurched out of my chest, stomach lodged in my throat, and I was given a head's up. Boss man slammed the brakes down – we were on a desolate highway – and screamed like a Banshee! The guy in the passenger seat flailed awake, thinking he's in the midst of a horrific accident. He braced the windshield with all fours – seat belt holding the rest of him back.

It was too dark to see if he dirtied his pants when he got out. I certainly bent a knee and said my prayers when I reached the safety of home. But I have to admit, I laughed pretty hard that day.

Mamu

I was always an early riser. When I slept in a strange bed, I'd rise even earlier. So it was when I spent the weekend at my mother- and father-in-laws' house.

Familiar with the layout of the house, I walked into the kitchen to get myself a cup of coffee after retrieving the newspaper out front. Before I sat down, I had to clear a spot to open the paper. The kitchen table sat four but the table was stacked high with books, magazines, archeological stuff and other research. It was typical for the amount of collecting they did. The clutter was extreme.

Once I settled in, sipped my coffee and found a good read, I enjoyed the silence of the wee hours – until a faint rustling noise caught my attention. I raised my head. Then, the hair on my neck felt like it stood straight up. To say I was startled would be an understatement.

Directly across from me was a tiny, frail woman, well into her 90s, with bug-eyed glasses, peering at me through the clutter.

It was "Mamu."

She had blended in so much, I never noticed her. Yet, she was up before me. Maybe she never went to sleep. Maybe she slept where she sat.

203

I still wanted to flee!

Before I could make a break for it, she spoke in Langish, alternating sentences between Latvian and English, "Good morning. Jums ir līdz agri līdzīgi man." So, I heard, "Good morning ...man."

Good enough. I returned the greeting of the day while I racked my brain for a reason to excuse myself. Unfortunately, my mental powers lay in the nearly full cup of coffee cooling before me.

"When I was a meitene Latvijā ..."

I knew I was trapped.

Twenty minutes went by and I was so confused. My attention span had met its limit 20 times over. I made occasional loud noises hoping to wake another house guest, preferrably my wife so I could slip away.

Mamu's crackly voice continued. Her head barely cleared the tabletop, blending into the stacks of who-knows-what lying everywhere.

Another 15 minutes dragged by before words I recognized like "jail, freed and fled the valsts," – well okay; "jail, free and fled" – raised my eyebrows.

Then a strange thing happened. I leaned in.

Not only that, I said, "Repeat that part again." ..."No, in English."

TWO HOURS LATER, I was hanging on her every word, whether it was in English or Latvian. It was World War II. Mamu, her husband and four – now five – young daughters were roaming war-torn Europe, homeless. A wagon wheel broke, they missed a boat, it was bombed and sunk. They slept in a farmer's field and woke to a glow of fire consuming the house they had been invited to sleep

204

in. There was a train they missed, a bomb, and I didn't need to translate the Latvian, I knew what happened next.

Someone walked by me, said, "Mornin'," and turned on the TV, ending one of the best stories I had ever heard.

Cara-boo

Our daughter was born around Halloween so we nicknamed her Cara-boo, a take on the word caribou. From the get-go, she gave us some scares.

My wife, Becky, had labor pains that began Sunday night and lasted until Tuesday evening. It was difficult to be bed side and watch my wife in such pain as I held her hand. I secretly wished for the old-fashioned days when the daddy-to-be could just pace the waiting room with a pocket full of cigars at the ready.

Although the nurse kept her cool, we knew something serious was happening. The baby's heart rate plunged. The nurse scrambled to find the doctor but he wasn't even on the floor. It was the middle of the night. I looked at Becky and could tell she was thinking the worst and on the verge of tears. She had previously had a miscarriage and that was after years of trying to get pregnant. The nurse had to go it alone so she reached inside to tickle the baby's head. It worked. The baby's heart rate picked up. I had every intention of writing a wonderful letter to that nurse but regret never following through. She was incredible.

My mom grew restless in the waiting room, seeing similarities to her problem delivery when I was born Cesarean. Back then, only one doctor at the hospital, fresh out of school, was available to do the procedure. Becky's long and complicated delivery made my mom's nerves hit the limit. She did what she does in times of crisis and took action. She bolted into the room, startling all of us.

"That's it! You get the doctor in here right now! It's time for a..." As Mom shouted more instructions, nurses escorted her back to the waiting area. Becky and I looked at each other and laughed – hard.

After Becky gave birth, I cut the umbilical cord. Then, our daughter was cradled by a completely depleted but glowing new mom. I stopped to think: Prior to that moment, much as I tried, I'd look at Becky and could not imagine her as a mother. Now, I looked at her and couldn't imagine her anything else. There they were, two beautiful angels, cuddled. Even though the journey was tough, our newborn came into the world perfect, like a porcelain doll. When our son was born a few years later, the delivery went much easier yet he came out looking like he had caught the bad end of a prize-fight.

Being our first child and living far from family and friends, Becky hardly had a support network. Making matters worse, our baby girl was colic. She also caught an infant respiratory virus. One night we drove to the emergency room because her breathing was so labored. Later, she was prescribed an inhaler and medicines for asthma.

All through my childhood, my parents would bark, "you'll get pneumonia dressed like that."

In college, too, my friends and I would jokingly bark at each other when someone was slow in shutting the door in winter – "Shut that pneumonia hole will ya."

Yet, I never knew anyone who actually had pneumonia ...until my son came back from the pediatrician with that diagnosis. It wasn't a big deal and he rebounded quickly. Then, we noticed our first grade daughter, Cara, experiencing a rapid fluttering in her chest. Becky took her immediately to the Urgicare center. Upon arrival, our little girl's heart rate plummeted and she turned gray. Next, she was rushed by ambulance to Children's Hospital in downtown Cincinnati. During that time, she was stabilized. At the hospital, it again got scary as her heart rate and oxygen levels plunged to life threatening lows.

She was recovering when I arrived. I don't know what my little girl was on but she was peppy as all get out. She spoke a million miles per second telling me all the cool things about the place, pointing at this and that, explaining with great exuberance – and then she said, "...And if I click this the nurse comes in," and the nurse came in.

By the time our son was in school, he had been to the hospital a few times with head injuries. Once, he fell off the top of a jungle-gym right in front of me, breaking his fall with his face. Blood gushed everywhere. As Becky came running across the soccer field and caught sight of all the blood, she nearly fainted. Many parents offered cloths of all sorts to help soak up the mess. Other than a broken nose and some stitches, he was okay. Another time, he stood on a swinging bench thinking he could do a cartwheel across it like a Power Ranger, but he flipped over the back and did a face plant into concrete. Imagine our self-consciousness as parents whose kids were prone to visits to the ER. We figured we had met our quota for a lifetime but as fate would have it, there was one more visit to go.

Our daughter, Cara, was now in elementary school and playing on a softball team. Becky and I set up our lawn chairs and talked with other parents as the kids went through pre-game warm-up drills. The assistant coach had them in a line as he hit balls for them to field. The girl in front of Cara was older, bigger and much better than the rest. The coach hit a liner that screamed off the bat so fast, the girl in front of Cara didn't want anything to do with it so she ducked to get out of its way. Cara took it straight in the eye and dropped like a sack of potatoes. At least that's what witnesses said. Becky and I weren't watching.

"Aww. Looks like someone got hurt," I said looking up to see what the emergency was.

"Is that Cara?" Becky tried to focus her eyes out on the field.

The coach frantically waved for me to come over. I waved him off as if to say, no worries, she'll shake it off. I didn't want to be the parent who runs out on the field because their baby got a boo-boo. I didn't know the severity. He waved again with a seriousness that couldn't be denied. Well, it was serious all right, serious enough where Cara spent the rest of the day undergoing medical tests.

Fortunately, it didn't break her eye socket. But she had the best shiner on her eye I had ever seen. The bruising went so deep, it took more than nine months before her skin tone completely returned to normal. She got the black eye in early spring and when she returned to school in the fall, it was still a black eye. As a parent, you couldn't help but wonder what teachers may have been thinking.

Fortunately, other than our son sticking a plastic bead down his ear canal and a plastic fork into the wall socket, things quieted down.

Scarred for Life

I was home alone with my pre-school daughter and toddler son, Cara and Dominic. It was an unseasonably beautiful day so I took them out to play in the driveway.

Dominic, a wobbly new walker, kept heading toward the lip along the upper edge of the drive where the concrete met gravel in a turnaround I just made. I knew he'd fall if he took one step over the lip. Like a magnet, no matter where I placed him, he drifted over there. My warnings grew sterner until I determined, fine, you'll learn on your own.

Sure enough, like a drunken sailor, Dominic wandered to the edge again. I waited for him to stumble and fall and he did.

He cried at the top of his lungs so I walked toward him waiving my finger saying, "I told you so," and then stopped cold.

His little baby-face looked up in horror. I instantly went bug-eyed.

There was a lot of blood.

I didn't understand how such a small fall could end so badly. I figured he'd plop on his butt and cry but this? He fell face-first onto a sharp piece of gravel – so sharp it went straight through the skin between his upper lip and nose.

There was a lot of blood – and blood curdling screaming.

I tucked him under my arm like a football and ran to the kitchen in our bi-level home. That meant upstairs. My innocent little daughter was in hot pursuit, obviously concerned and confused at what was happening. My voice had a tone of panic as I talked out loud trying to sooth my boy. My girl stood in the kitchen with her baby doll strapped to her front, trying to process the scene.

I turned on the faucet and dunked Dominic's face into the running water to wash away the blood so I could see how badly he was cut and where. His wailing was deafening. As I held him in the sink, legs flailing upward in the air, I noticed the gawking of neighbors working in their backyards. Their sights were locked on me through the open upper window right over my kitchen sink.

Then, "DADDY-DADDY-DON'T DO BAD THINGS TO DOMINIC! DADDY-DADDY-DON'T DO BAD THINGS TO DOMINIC! DADDY-DADDY-DON'T DO BAD THINGS TO DOMINIC!" over and over and over.

This plea from my horrified little girl pierced all other noise. I knew she was heard, plain as day, across the neighborhood.

There I was with my boy's head under the faucet water, feet flailing in the air and neighbors gawking in alarm as my daughter's voice cut through the air with confusion and panic, "DADDY-DADDY-DON'T DO BAD THINGS TO DOMINIC!"

Later, the pediatrician said Dominic was too young for the wound to leave a scar, but he was wrong.

The only question now is whose scar runs deeper.

Elian Gonzalez

I come from a family who hold strong opinions. I married into a family who also hold strong opinions. If you say black, someone is bound to say white, down to your up, or sideways just to mess with your head.

Conversations often became debates and sometimes, debates turned into arguments. It could be politics, sports, current affairs or how efficiently you just loaded the dish washer. Someone was always there to one-up and show they know best. And we all loved this "entertainment" in matching wit.

Things went a step further in the controversy surrounding Elian Gonzalez.

Elian Gonzalez was a little Cuban boy who washed ashore, tragically, without his mother. His father wanted him back. His Florida relatives said no. Should he stay or should he go? That was the international headline for months! If you listened long enough to the warring sides, you were sure to pick one. It could range on personal feelings, family views, patriotism, and honestly being torn about what was right for the child.

My wife and I sat down in a restaurant, along with extended family members. The room was big. We were out in the open, at tables pulled together to accommodate our party. Before we ordered, the rhetoric heat was ratcheting up quickly. Everyone had done their homework. All parties knew this would be a topic of discussion. It was difficult to breakaway to give the waitress our menu orders. When we unclicked the uncomfortable pause button, each of us chomping at the bit to say our piece on the matter, the exchange quickly transgressed from conversation to a knife fight with sharp words. It was clear, there were two uncompromising parties well prepared to influence the opposition come hell or high water. Everyone was guilty.

But two in particular drowned out the others – one was me. As the kids of the time would say – it was on!

We were factual. We were philosophical. We were loud!

It was personal.

My "opponent" had had enough, stood, tossed his napkin down and headed for the door.

Shocked silence filled the table.

I gave chase offering peace. I still offered it in the parking lot as he drove away. There was simply too much steam to cool.

What happened? I was embarrassed. I walked back inside and the rest of the family was stunned when I said he wasn't coming back.

Somewhere along the way or maybe all along, a debate over the issue of the day became a heart-felt, passionate declaration. I didn't recognize that at the time. It's one thing to argue with someone when it's a chess match of wit but quite another matter when the heart of a lion comes into play. The right thing to do in that situation, unless you're equally passionate in your heart of hearts, is stand down.

That didn't happen and now there was a price to pay even for the innocent bystanders.

We returned back at my "opponent's" house where calmer nerves prevailed. My "opponent" casually prepared wild mushrooms for a snack without offering much to say. He had picked his own. Anyone who knows anything about mushrooms knows that improper identification can be fatal.

"No-no, Rocky, these over here I picked special for you."

Pastime

When I was 7-years-old, Dad took Grandpa and me to a ballgame. It was my first.

Grandpa told me how he fell in love with the sport when he was around my age, several years after emigrating from Sicily. Dad went to get some foot longs and I sat there next to my grandpa, holding onto my little league glove. I heard the crack of the bat and saw the ball coming closer – Closer – CLOSER. We were in the upper deck down the third base line. When that ball whizzed directly over my head I yanked back my outstretched glove because I wanted no part of it.

I shook Grandpa afterward and screamed, "Did you see that!"

He grunted, "See what, see what?"

He had no clue what just happened. Little did he know that was the moment I became a fan of the game and his team, just like my father before me.

Decades later, it was time to pass down the family tradition.

My daughter, Cara, was only 4-years-old and we were going to move away because of a job offer. Before we left, I wanted to take my little girl to experience the magic of Jacob's Field.

We got on what Cara called "the train ride" and settled into a seat that happened to face backward. She liked that. I didn't.

The man sitting in front of us had big hair.

"Dad – look, that man has a comb stuck in his head."

I saw the big hair shift but not make a complete turn.

After that, we arrived, stood at the end of the line and walked into the ballpark.

I don't give my kids a lot by today's standards but I flat out spoiled my daughter on that day. Program – yes. Hot dog – yes. Peanuts – yes. Cracker Jack – yes. After all this and three innings, Cara saw a man with a big tray of clouds on sticks, colors dancing in the light one section over. She followed him with her eyes. Finally, she asked about this strange sight. Now, her only mission in life was to try this thing called cotton candy.

Half an inning later, she was twisted backward, thumping my shoulder without looking, as she panted, "He's coming, Dad. Dad, here he comes."

I decided to make her earn this treat and said that she had to get his attention to come down to us or she would be out of luck.

She asked how to do it so I told her to just yell, "Cotton Candy here!"

So she did! LOUDLY and REPEATEDLY.

Seeing how she handled the entire transaction by herself, many in our section gave her a standing ovation.

Her head swelled.

I had to tilt my head back to contain the pooling water building up in my eyes.

When the game was over, we soaked in the experience for a while longer until we were one of the last there.

"Dad, I love our team. Did they win?"

"I'll always remember this day too, honey."

Achieving My American Dream

There were naysayers – and there were plenty of them – before I took the entrepreneurial plunge.

Having worked myself up the corporate ladder to Director of Marketing and Public Relations for the parent company, I knew they were going to close operations in Hudson, Ohio where I worked. Rather than relocate out-of-state and away from family, I signed what was called a stay-put package to remain through the transition to ensure it went smoothly. This stay-put package, my normal pay and bonus, and a generous severance package allowed me the luxury to take some time off and write a book while I sought a new employer. In the meantime, I "stayed put" for a year. I brushed up my resume and acquired new skills, including how to build a web site. Once the web site was in place, my PR savvy was put to work.

Not being able to afford advertising for my web site, I created homemade bumper stickers, which lasted until the first rain. Then, living on a busy – former country – road in Strongsville, Ohio, I created a homemade billboard for my front yard. Neighbors loved it I'm sure. It lasted until the next rain, which wasn't long. But, lots of people started visiting the site. Then, I got creative – or quirky – and devised some things that grabbed media attention.

Spot-The-Rock was the first idea to catch hold in a big way. He was a throwback to the pet-rock craze of the 1970s. However he weighed about 20 pounds, not including his wagon. He had eyes, long hair, arms and legs (taken from one of the kids' dolls along with a voice box). Spot became a sensation and was booked across Northeast Ohio to make appearances, meet kids and talk about travel and safety. After several other gimmicks and modest news coverage, I discovered a part of the web site was fast becoming a favorite – free places to travel around Northern Ohio.

By this time, I was out of work and also interested in free Ohio fun to entertain my family of four. Finding so many free things to do and places to go, statewide, I decided to write a book about it. Then, the entire web site was channeled to promote the book. Before it was printed (self-published after numerous rejections), I had a job-offer in Cincinnati and went through the pains of selling our home and relocating my family.

Between houses, we had two apartments. One was short-term housing provided complimentary by my new employer along with a signing bonus. Within the next six months, we'd call four places home. On a mini trip, my children looked at our hotel room and asked if it was our home now.

Eighteen months later, book sales produced a little extra money. Managing to get my book in major bookstores, libraries and online sellers, resulted in about a dozen book signings. This meant sitting in a chair at a table and watching people walk by wondering who the hell I was.

More importantly, the web site had acquired a rather large audience – probably because it was cross promoted with the book. This prompted the biggest sales presentation of my life; not to corporate leaders, bankers or investors but to my wife! I had an entrepreneurial idea and asked her to just give me six months to make something happen. If it didn't work, I'd have time to find a new job, hopefully. Oh, and if I couldn't pull it off, we risked having to spend our savings to get by. But to do this right and have a chance, I needed to go at it full-time. She reluctantly agreed to the risks in my start-up venture.

My expansion of OhioTraveler.com offered unique family attractions across the state and not just the freebies from the book. Even though book sales were still going well, I made the decision to dump its entire content into the web site, offering it for free. I also used the site as a tool to develop a marketing practice that helped those in the tourism field that the larger firms ignored – organizations with little to no budgets.

My first client was a non-profit in the poorest county in Ohio, smack in the foothills of Appalachia. It came by way of a direct marketing email campaign followed up by a cold-call. One of my first promotional campaigns for a client involved getting media and online attention for what are known as quilt barns or barn quilt squares. It was a hit. Today, quilt barns dot the countryside throughout the Midwest and beyond. So, a seed was planted and I was fortunate to harvest many new clients through word-of-mouth coming from this critical early success.

The road I chose to travel had its share of bumps and fear of failure. It was a roller coaster. The most difficult part was not having a routine paycheck. I can't tell you how many times I thought I might end up peeing blood from the stress of providing for my wife and children. But, I stuck with it and my wife stuck with me, whispering confidence in my ear when I needed it most.

We had no money for extras. Renting videos and ordering pizza were beyond our budget. My wife said we could use a bookcase so I built one – a pretty big one – out of wood. What it taught us was how to appreciate what we had. But what I rediscovered most was what had been long lost – personal freedom! Gone were the days I'd only see my children an hour before bedtime during the week. Now, I worked from home. Coupled with my wife – a special education teacher – we had much needed flexibility in our schedules. Three years later, we were earning money beyond what was needed to just get by.

OhioTraveler.com grew to attract one of the largest audiences of any magazine online or in print in the state, topping 18 million hits per year by more than one million visitors.

I self-taught myself many things, including shooting and editing video for clients. This service would grow to become half of my business. I had never done it before but figured my creativity and general know-how would be enough to do a decent job.

After landing my first paid shoot, I stood on a sidewalk, watching my new client walk toward me. I started sweating bullets because I couldn't remember how to turn the camera on. But, the video turned out nicely and she used it for years. Eventually, a client won awards for a video I shot.

I continued on with innovative ideas to capture media attention. Some of my bigger successes were called GraveQuest, The Boneheaded Tourist and Lost in Ohio. It propelled me to regular guest appearances on television morning shows in Cincinnati and Columbus. I also landed interviews by other television, radio, newspapers and magazines, some even national in scope.

Sometimes I became overwhelmed with fear because I handled everything in the business by myself and the competition had grown fierce. Other times, I'd sit back and just smile at what I had pulled off. It was refreshing and rewarding to pursue a dream and succeed on my terms, persevering through my self-doubt and growing pains.

It wasn't easy but I had somehow achieved my American dream.

Deceiving the Innocent

One Christmas, when I was a kid, I hid behind the living room couch hoping to sneak a peek at Santa Claus. It was long after my bedtime. I dozed off.

When I awoke, I only saw feet from my vantage point. Something was wrong. Santa was wearing slippers. I stretched to see the figure putting gifts under the Christmas tree. My world crashed!

I think my daughter, Cara, was the most crushed I had ever seen a kid learning there was no Santa. But that wouldn't be the biggest or longest lasting deceit she'd fall victim to.

When Cara was a preschooler, she drew up elaborate treasure maps with her magic markers. We would go through the house together, following these maps to see where they led. On the first nice spring day of the year, she showed me her latest treasure map and I decided to play it up big-time. We followed the map she made. Then I mentioned certain imagery matched certain landmarks and she agreed. This took us outside on a great adventure. She rolled with it.

"This dotted line here and that scribble up there – that must mean we follow the stone steps down to the bushes by the creek," I said. "Does it look that way to you?"

She agreed.

"I can't figure this part out, where do you think it goes?" I asked.

Cara was full swing into a great adventure by now.

"Dad, this must lead up to the old cemetery." She was in control.

We zigzagged through the woods, back and forth over the creek, and finally to some old headstones.

"Look, this guy was born before the Revolutionary War!" I said.

"What's the Wewutionry Board?"

"It means it's old – very old – so old I wonder if he wrote the treasure map."

"Dad, I drew it!"

"Oh-ya, where to next?"

Looking at the last scribble, I told Cara where I thought it led. She didn't disagree – already a step ahead in her thinking that maybe something could actually be there. I sunk the shovel into the dirt. I made her dig, too, when I got tired.

It dawned on me that earlier I had been standing in a cemetery with a shovel on my shoulder.

Low and behold, Cara's shovel hit a container. Her eyes lit up so bright I reached for my sunglasses on top of my head. We pulled out and opened a dirty "treasure chest."

She screamed in delight at the things we found inside.

Cara ran up the hill, through the backyard and into the house – beaming – to show her mommy.

Years later, my wife, Becky, was driving Cara and her teenage friends to go shopping. They were talking about the things they believed in when they were younger, like Santa Claus. They also talked about some other incredulous stuff and that's when Cara shared her true story of miraculously discovering a treasure through a map she drew.

"I mean, to this day, I still can't believe it. Like, how was that even possible?" Cara asked.

The car fell silent.

"Uh, Cara, Dad buried that," Becky chuckled, amazed that Cara still believed this was a real life event, especially coming from an honor student in all advanced classes.

Pause.

"Wait! What?"

And another lie to a kid was exposed, albeit well past its expiration date.

Spring Break for Old Dudes

Spring break means different things to different people in different stages of life. For me, as a middle-aged man, married with two young children, it meant a long weekend getaway for Easter break with family and friends.

Every January my friend Mike and I get both of our families together for a three night stay in a nice large cabin with a hot tub somewhere in Ohio. But for whatever reasons, this time January drifted into February and then March. So we decided since both of our wives were teachers, we'd book a place over their spring break. That way, the wives and kids all had time off. Perfect.

When we arrived, it was not what we had expected. First lesson; don't trust what you see online. It was a mini cabin in the woods, located on a cul-de-sac road, and nearby a lake. The surrounding cabins were bursting at the seams with college kids on SPRING BREAK! That is, every cabin but ours and as I would later learn, one somewhere across the street.

Mike was unusually quiet as we drank some beer and fired up the grill. Bon Jovi music was bouncing off the trees all around us. I guess that's what the "kids" considered *classic rock* these days. The only good thing was that these small cabins somehow had thick enough walls, soundproofed enough, to block out the noise from the all night partying going on next door. Fortunately there was a vacant, tree-filled lot separating us. We decided to brave the night and express our disappointment to management at the main lodge in the morning since it was already getting late and the kids were ready for sleep. Our kids that is!

Stepping out back, Mike and I drank beer a little faster than we had in a long time. That's when "Mr. Buff" appeared. Buff had a chiseled …everything. I tried to stick out my chest but realized it was left behind in Germany when I was in the Army years ago. Either that or the good life had grown my stomach.

Anyway, Mr. Buff said, "We were talking over there and decided, ya know what? Let's give these old-dudes our cell phone number so if they need us to pump down the volume, we'll know."

I was puzzled and looked around for these old dudes. It was like a truck hit me when I realized Buff was referring to us! He was so nice though, in that fake, but believing he was sincere, kind of way.

I kept having visions of us being in the middle of one of those insurance commercials – "LIFE! It Comes At You Fast!"

Well, inside the cabin, all things were quiet – proof that miracles do exist.

The next day, we did some sightseeing, ate lunch at a nice place and then someone suggested we go antiquing.

Although I wanted to, something inside me screamed, "Noooo!"

So after we spent two hours in the antique mall, we went to the lodge, swam, played games and had a fine time. On the way out, we stopped at the front desk and said we hoped there would be patrols to keep the college kids at bay, but that there were no complaints at this time.

We drove back to "cul-de-sac Ft. Lauderdale" to see nearly every rooftop shingled with girls in bikinis and guys with no shirts. Below, there was a wiffle-ball game going on at the end of the cul-de-sac. Our kids asked if they could play too. Yeah right.

At dusk, I had to take some trash to a nearby dumpster. There were raccoons. Yippee! So I got the kids, walked back and showed them "wildlife." After the little scavengers entertained us, it grew darker so we headed back to the cabin.

Fortunately, only I saw the streaking from afar. At least this night, the party was at the cabin across the street instead of next door. Things were definitely getting wilder.

In the morning, we decided we'd had enough. After packing the van I had to make another walk to the dumpster. On my way back, I was startled to see a family of four emerge from a cabin kitty-corner from ours and next door to last night's party.

Here's their story:

"In the middle of the night, my worst fear came true," said kitty-corner dad. "Someone was banging on the back door yelling, *let me in.* I yelled back, You better get out of here, this isn't your cabin, now go away. To which the drunk on the other side pleaded, *Come on dude, stop mess'n with my head and just let me in.* This repeated a few times before the stranger at the door fell silent."

And so it goes.

I could tell us "old dudes" had a new story to tell.

Going Postal

I was suited with a heart-vest to monitor my ticker for 24 hours. Little plastic cups and wires were suctioned and taped all over my torso. I hated it.

As the doctor directed, I proceeded with my normal routine, except, this would be an abnormal day. The kids had a day off school yet I still needed to work, albeit from my home office. I was uncomfortable and very conscious of the Frankenstein concoction rubbing under my loosely fitted shirt. I was sensitive.

My pre-school son was in a stage where he'd run up and slam into me, sometimes wrapping his arms and legs around me. Already irritable, this aggravated me more. I was afraid he'd rip a wire off and then what? Start another 24-hour period from scratch I assumed.

"Stop it!"

An hour later, "Stop it, I mean it this time!"

Thirty more minutes go by, "I SAID STOP IT, OR-OR-I'LL TAKE YOUR TOYS AWAY."

Finally, I just needed to get out of the house so I finished preparing a bunch of boxes for a marketing mailing and headed for the post office, kids in tow.

My timing was awful. The line was backed up. The kids were antsy.

Standing there with boxes stacked up chest high on my dolly, I did a slow boil every time the little bugger smacked into me. Although red in the face, I waited, patiently. Actually, impatiently!

Then, a post office worker closed his station and disappeared into the back leaving one guy to handle a long line. Every minute ticked by like an eternity.

Finally, it was my turn.

I rolled my boxes up to the counter and communicated calmly how to send them. One by one, I reached down, carefully, so I wouldn't tear off any wires hidden under my shirt. While bent over, a 3-foot fleshy tank rammed into me and reached around my body in a death grip!

Standing up, I looked at my son and said for all to hear, "Stop running into me, YOU KNOW I HAVE WIRES ALL OVER MY BODY!"

You could hear a pin drop.

Topino

The tooth fairy is a celebrated legend in much of the world. So, too, is the tooth mouse.

226

My dad was born to a Sicilian immigrant. Growing up, my dad and his siblings were told of "the little white tooth mouse." Instead of a tooth fairy, it was a tooth mouse who would appear at night to exchange the baby tooth for a coin.

Although Dad shared his childhood tale of the tooth mouse with my sister and me, we went with the American standard – the tooth fairy.

When I had kids of my own, I decided to reintroduce the tooth mouse tradition of my dad's childhood, but with a twist. First, I discovered the tooth mouse went by different names throughout the world. In Italian, the name was Topino.

I told my kids that when their grandpa was a kid, there was a mouse in his house named Topino. Topino emmigrated from Sicily with the Satullo family. His job was to check the childrens' teeth every night and when he found a wiggler, he'd put the tooth fairy on high alert. She was very busy so it was helpful to have a tooth mouse in the house. He would give her a head's up so she could better plan her route each night. A tooth would be exchanged with a coin by the tooth mouse and a dollar bill by the tooth fairy. When kids grew up, so did their tooth mouse. The tooth mouse would have baby mice, all named Topino. When the kids started their own families, a Topino would move in with each of them.

My son, Dominic, not only believed in Topino, he was so fascinated by this peculiar mouse, he took things to a new level. One night, my wife came into our room after replacing the tooth with a coin and bill and handed me a note. Our son was asking the tooth mouse questions like what does he

227

look like, where does he live, what else did he like to do, and can he read this?

So began a strange pen pal relationship between my son and me. Our minds worked together to open a whole new world. It didn't matter if a tooth was loose or not, I had to check his desk to see if a letter was left for Topino. The fun wrapped around this communication between father and son was something for the ages. There were great adventures, head-scratching questions, revelations and more.

One of Dominic's favorite storylines revolved around the mischief Topino got into at night when he'd play with Dominic's toys. One time we awoke to a toy car stuck in the chandelier. Don't ask, it's a long story! Topino also seemed to get into the same life situations as my son, at the same time, so it became the topic of conversation between them. Until one day it stopped.

We had carried on the letter writing for a couple of years. Sure, there were some long pauses at times between letters so when they stopped altogether, I was slow to notice. Finally, I asked Dominic if he still left letters for Topino. He showed me the last letter he wrote that had gone unanswered.

"Why did you put it here?" I asked, aware that it was not the usual spot.

"I don't know," he answered.

Since it was not in the assumed usual spot, I explained that Topino may have missed the note. Dominic then moved the note to the old spot. But there was more to Topino not finding the letter than it just being in the wrong spot. Topino, too, had been in the wrong spot.

Dominic ran downstairs the next morning with a wad of papers in hand.

"Look – look, Topino, he's back!"

"Whattaya mean, back?" I asked coyly.

"He hid in my bag the last time we went to Avon Lake to visit. It took him forever to get back and he waited a long time after that for me to write him. He didn't know I did because I used a different spot for the letter so you were right about that, Dad. I can't wait to hear about his adventure!"

So there were stories that lasted another year.

Then one day Dominic looked on in horror as I put out mouse poison in the garage, cautioning him to stay clear of it. I had to convince him that I bought a special blend that targeted unwanted mice versus a beloved tooth mouse like Topino. He preferred all mice live. I had other ideas considering the bag of seed they feasted on all winter.

Eventually, it ended as most childhood fairytales end; by just growing too old to believe anymore.

Feelin' "The Heat!"

I was in a melancholy mood when I went to the post-office. I had to pay a speeding ticket I received in a little town in Illinois named Galena. I was convinced that I was a victim of a speed trap. However, I was sure there would be hell-to-pay if I challenged this officer after what I had unknowingly done to him.

Our family of four was on the first-day drive of our vacation across the country. After high winds and plenty of ugly gray windmill farms throughout

Indiana and Illinois, we were happy to be closing in on our first destination. The road was winding through trees, up and down hilly countryside, when I saw the new speed limit sign. It was about the same time a patrol car passed from the opposite direction. I didn't see the cruiser brake, slow or turnaround through my rear-view mirror. We rounded the bend and turned the music back up.

The GPS was providing our navigation and we were listening to the MP3 playing Holiday Road by Lindsey Buckingham – a fitting song if you ever saw National Lampoon's Vacation. Bobbing our heads and singing along, we drove over a hill and became mesmerized by a picturesque town ahead.

The hillside view of Galena was just gorgeous!

Our vehicle echoed with, "Look at THIS town, check out the building over there, no –look at that, we need a picture."

The spontaneity quickly turned to, "Stop there, no –turn there, turn again, WAIT! There's a cop behind us with his lights on."

I pulled into a roadside parking space as I replayed our course in my mind. All I could imagine was that I must have rolled through a stop sign.

I rolled my window down, feeling the heat and precipitation only it had nothing to do with the muggy weather. This officer was in my ear, spitting and shouting like a drill sergeant would to a new recruit.

"Don't they pull over to the right in Ohio!" he hollered. It wasn't a question.

I thought for sure this guy was gasoline and I was a lit match so I proceeded with caution and kindness. But he'd have none of it, except my license, registration and proof of insurance.

He remained livid and shouted plenty more before storming back to his cruiser.

Then, we waited …and waited …and waited.

Meanwhile, I had to explain to my nine-year-old daughter and seven-year-old son that their dad was not going to jail (at least I didn't think I was) but was most definitely going to get a ticket. My mind drifted to paying a fine and whether or not my insurance rate would go up. What a way to blow the budget on the first day of vacation!

The policeman returned and the puzzle pieces fell into place. Here, it turned out he had been in the cop car I thought didn't turn around wa-a-a-ay back on that country road. Now I'm not sure if he ever had his siren on because the music wasn't THAT loud. The kids would have complained otherwise. His flashing light was not one mounted to the exterior of the car. Rather it was flashing from the interior. The officer ensued in what was a low-speed-chase covering a couple miles, by my estimation. The cop was convinced he was "chasing" defiant tourists, when in actuality our attention had been bent on taking photographs.

Ticket apparent, I said as little as I had to when he returned to my window.

Later, I read in a magazine that Galena was one of the hundred places I must see before I die.

And we never did take a picture of it!

Mount Cr@p Your Pants

Hmmm. I was going to take the long way around until a park ranger challenged my manhood back at Natural Bridges National Monument. I had asked her if the Moki Dugway posed any danger. You know because of the kids and all.

She looked me straight in the eyes and actually said, "Take off the skirt."

Nuff said. We're doing it.

As I sat, stopped, pulled off the road, staring at an intimidating sign warning what's ahead, I looked at my wife riding shotgun and the kids through the rear-view mirror. We still had a choice, drive the long way around a mountain or go over the top of it. The problem with going over it was that it was described as having a steep, narrow, dirt, switch-back road without guard rails and a maximum speed limit of five miles per hour.

I was still thinking about the death defying cliff drive we experienced just a week earlier when we rolled up to the Yellowstone gate at dusk. On that day, we were alone except for one ranger in one booth. I got to flash my national parks pass for the second time that day. I couldn't help but smile.

The Yellowstone ranger said we came at the perfect time. I asked why. He said this road had been closed all afternoon because of the snow but had just reopened 30 minutes ago. Then he made an offer we should have refused. He said from what he was hearing, the road could be closed again in as little as 15 minutes so if we're going, we'd better go now.

Somewhere inside of me, I was naïvely thinking if there's any real danger, a ranger would never …

Yellowstone's East Entrance was along a steep cliff down on the left and up on the right. The right side of the road at least had a pitch to it, but the left side was a straight drop to a bottom, too far to see. The music was off. Nobody so much as whispered except for an occasional gasp. Then our bodies stiffened!

YIKES!

Snow drifted over our lane as high as our vehicle, leaving the slightest space in the opposing lane to maneuver around it. As if that weren't bad enough, there were no guard rails. Just when we thought it couldn't get any worse, the road was icy. We couldn't have turned around if we wanted. Driving in reverse was out of the question. If we stopped, I was afraid the vehicle would slide off the edge. So we crept ever so slowly into the opposite lane, careful not to look over the bare edge. My knuckles were as white as the landscape. My wife was clutching the dashboard and the kids had closed their eyes, sensing imminent danger. These driving conditions continued for such a long time, I wondered if we'd ever make it.

"STOP!"

In the middle of the road, there was a bison blanketed in snow. We thread the needle of the large animal on the side with the snow drift and the sheer death plunge on the other side.

"Please Mr. Buffalo; do NOT nudge us in any way."

My wife snapped me back to the present situation, "Are you going or not?"

233

I phoned a friend who had come this way in the past.

"Mike, did you go on this dirt road over mount...?"

"If you don't go over it, you will miss some of the most spectacular views," he deadpanned.

Queuing up Pink Floyd's *Learning to Fly*, we ascended into the sky when I thought *The Turning Away* may have been the more appropriate song choice.

This was one speed limit I certainly would not break. Once we were clearly at breakneck heights I felt like I was hyperventilating ...just a little bit.

The kids loved it.

They also loved my fear. "Dad, how fast would we hit bottom if the edge of the road crumbles around this next turn?"

"QUIET! Let me concentrate!" I was serious.

Meanwhile, my wife was busy taking pictures and some out-of-focus video. Her sound effects were in awe of the incredible views; she kept pointing as if I was supposed to look.

Going up I had to drive on the outer part of the 1 ½ lane road. As long as there weren't any cars coming from the other direction, I was able to hug the rock wall on the inner part of the lane, still being very conscious of the slight dirt embankment separating us from a death fall.

There were times when I, too, got swept up in the amazing breadth of scenery the closer we got to the summit. It was like looking out of an airplane window (except when rock cliffs were in my peripheral vision) and seeing a ribbon of road stretching for what might have been a hundred miles. Perhaps I'm slightly exaggerating but it was a sight to behold.

"CAR," shouted my wife.

"Holy %&#@!*^&%!" I countered.

We passed within inches of each other. I was maxing out at five miles per hour when they whizzed by doing at least 12 MPH – MORE THAN DOUBLE THE SPEED LIMIT.

Some people are just crazy.

Speaking to God

I was raised with faith in God and am at peace most when I am with nature. By no means am I a preachy person or some holy roller. People may even be surprised to hear of my religious convictions. In any case, I had been examining my thoughts about God, asking questions, and pondering a lot about why we exist, what happens next and a whole lot more but at one point, here's what happened. I talked to God and God, I believe, "talked to me." Stop laughing. It happened three times! I understand God works through nature in subtle and mysterious ways. So maybe I asked the right questions at the right times and opened my eyes to see the signs.

The first "conversation" came after I turned the dirt in the garden. I was thirsty so I walked briskly through the backyard to the house.

In a fraction of a second, my mind – out of the blue – thought, "God, show me a sign that you really are there, anything."

I was in full stride, thirsty. But at that very moment, I looked and stooped down in one smooth motion. I saw and picked a four leaf clover in the second it took.

Then I looked up to the sky and joked, "That was a good one."

My second "conversation" was also unexpected. I had just dropped the car off for repair early in the morning. The whole family was with me. My wife, Becky, had some errands to do with the kids. I was wearing sweat pants and sneakers so, compulsively, I decided to go for a run. I had not gone running in years. I had hiked, biked and walked plenty, but not run. Anyway, I wanted to drink in the morning air, exercise my body and breathe deeply. So we pulled the van over to a new shopping entrance that led to a trail that connected to Voice of America Park.

I stretched and ran.

The way I was supposed to go was blocked. Rather than turn back, I ran on through tall grass and weeds and even jumped a creek in order to get to an old paved road that lead to the lake and an asphalt running trail. When I got to the start of the loop trail around the lake, rain poured down. I had nowhere to go until Becky came back to pick me up. People – joggers and walkers – scrambled past me, in the opposite direction, to get to their cars in a nearby parking lot. I jogged on. Then, thunder and lightning delivered quite a scare. As I ran along the water's edge, I really thought there was a great chance I could actually be struck down by lightning. By this time, turning back was no shorter a distance than continuing around the loop trail.

Then, in the pouring rain, I stopped and looked down. I don't know why. And I picked up a tiny muddy cube. I rubbed it and saw that it was silver with a design but it was a quarter inch wide at best. It was really tiny and dirty, not at all shiny. I don't know how I had spotted it because it looked much like the scattered pebbles. But instead of pitching it back to the muddy ground, I put it in my pocket.

Later, at home, I showed Becky and she washed it off. She said that it looked like there was paper inside. I was in disbelief but the tiny cube had a side missing in which a two inch by two inch piece of paper was folded and jammed inside so tightly it was not wet at all. It wasn't dirty either.

We unfolded it together and here's what it said:

The Lord is my shepherd. I shall not
Want. He maketh me to lie down in
Green pastures: he leads me beside
The still water. He restores my soul.
And leads me in the path of righteous
Ness for his names sake. Yea, tho I
Walk through the valley of death, I
Will fear no evil, for thou art with me;
Thy rod and staff comfort me. Thou
Preparest a table before me in the
Presence of my enemies and anoint
My head with oil; my cup runneth
Over. Surely goodness and mercy
Shall follow me all the days of my
Life and I will dwell in the house of
The Lord forever.   Amen.

My last "conversation" with God came at my son's baseball practice. It was a cold and wet spring day. As the coaches and kids took the field, I walked around.

In a direct request, I said to God, "If you really are out there, let me find another four leaf clover."

I looked down, scanning the ground from a standing position. I saw it within seconds and picked it.

I continued to walk, not staying in any one area and not bending over too closely to examine clover patches, just walking and standing.

"Okay God, how about one four leaf clover for Cara, Dominic and Becky, too? That would be impressive."

Just like that, I had four – four-leaf clovers – in my hand.

I walked to the car and put the clovers inside and on the way back, I said to myself, "This is just crazy. One more. Just one more." And there it was.

Then, a little voice in my head – not really a voice but a thought – said, "That's it. That's all you get."

And as much as I searched, I never found another four-leaf clover.

Walkabout

Tucked deep in the Arts & Crafts district of Gatlinburg, we unpacked while marveling at the skyline of mountains piercing a low blanket of marshmallow clouds. Did someone say wine and hot tub? I did.

Meanwhile, my wife, Becky, got a case of the giggles as she rummaged through my backpack looking for something but found pepper spray, a bowie knife, a snake bite kit, an air horn, whistle, bells – oh, and a machete.

Becky couldn't stop laughing and mocking me.

On the defensive, I felt compelled to explain my survival tools. The snake bite kit was self-explanatory. It may surprise you that the knife and machete weren't for bear encounters. Rather, they were reserved for the psychopath roaming the Appalachian Trail. Like the Boy Scouts say, "Be prepared!" For the bear, I figured I'd use my blow horn to scare it away or pepper spray if it got too close.

Snow fell with darkness. We nestled by firelight reading about prospective trails we could explore at daybreak.

After we left Rainbow Falls and the tourists, we only saw one other person on the long ascent to summit Mount LeConte. It was a ranger who suggested we backtrack a bit to see a spectacular overlook. Our legs and feet were yearning for the summit and rest, but the view such as he described prevailed.

Although the detour wasn't that far, all said, it was far enough to hear my feet bark at me, "Why-whyy-whyyy…"

The swaths of greenery to our sides, stepping stones at our feet and canopy above all rose together to a blue sky at the end of nature's tunnel. It was a remarkable visual. Thank goodness film is obsolete because we would have used all that we had right here.

Afterward, we walked and talked, "This one or that one?" Delete. "This one or that one?" Delete. "This one or that one?" Decide later. "This one or that one?" Both.

Just a couple hundred feet from the summit was LeConte Lodge. There were also a bunch of tiny, weathered, wooden cabins or shacks and a small provisions store that offered hikers energy by the pound. It was an unusual, but welcome, sight. The tiny shacks provided the essentials; a roof over a bed and a tiny porch. The panoramic view made us wish we had a reservation.

Ironically, the question of the hour was, "Are you staying the night?"

Most people would spend the day hiking up and another day hiking down. We were the fools who thought we could do both in the same day. We contemplated the time it would take for our descent, using a different trail named Bullhead. The daylight hours were slipping away.

We topped off our water supply and checked out the small provisions store. I asked where I might find a rest room and the extremely friendly lady in the store pointed out the directions. I followed them until I was inside someone's shack. It was a little embarrassing. Tripping over myself, I scrambled over another row to find the potty-shack.

We chatted with some other hikers when it dawned on me, I don't think I've ever run into a non-friendly person on a trail. The irony of my machete poking me through my backpack struck me.

Relatively rejuvenated, we began down Bullhead. My shin splints and foot-aches shouted out, "Remember me – still here!"

It was just Becky and me so I complained aloud about my aching this and that. About an hour into the one-track conversation I realized what she was thinking of me. I spent the next hour trying to rationalize it. She had fun with me the whole time …at my expense.

Bullhead Trail was a backwoods paradise – not a soul on it except us. Trailside scenery and mountain ledge views made me think of becoming a mountain man – until I took my next step and found myself muzzling my pain.

"I hurt too but I just don't complain about it," Becky said, sarcasm dripping from the corners of her grin.

"Bear droppings."

I moved my pepper-spray and air horn to where I could easily grab them from the sides of my backpack.

Becky wasn't convinced but I saw more and more as we walked. We were definitely tracking a bear down this desolate path.

"What do I need to prove it – a bear?" I said in frustration.

"If you see one, just know that while you fumble with your weapons, I'll be running the other way," she joked …at least I thought she was joking. "Outrunning you shouldn't be difficult considering you're limping on bloody stumps to hear you go on about it."

So this was our memorable adventure. When we hit bottom, literally and figuratively – speaking for myself of course – my mind had prepared for the car to be right there. However, it was miles away so we had to trek yet another trail just to get back to where we had started.

It was dusk and even Becky was finally complaining of her own aches and pains and said we had pushed our limits too far. We were slap happy, laughing as if we were delirious, going on about our sore muscles and joints.

A funny thing happens when you walk as we did for an entire day up and down a mountain and then suddenly stop. And by stop I mean put our feet in the car and drive. When we put our feet back down at a restaurant parking lot, joints like knees didn't function like the brain intended. We both waddled on rubber legs into the restaurant determined to feast as a reward for our stupendous journey.

On our way out, having had nothing alcoholic to drink, two people wanted to get us a ride so we wouldn't drive. We were still wobbly and clutching each other to keep from collapsing, laughing hysterically at our zombie feet.

Everyone thought we were three sheets to the wind as we hobbled to our car, giddy as all get out, and waved goodbye.

Fly on the Wall

We were prudent when I experienced tightness in my chest, sharp pains and other symptoms I would normally sleep off as stress or strained muscles.

My wife, Becky, called her sister who said, "Best to bring him in."

She was a nurse at a nearby hospital and so was her husband. After we arrived at the Emergency Room, tests were done. Becky held my hand loyally by my side, concerned. I tried to lighten the mood with humor. In between my chest clutching jolts and long pauses, I tried to think of my next one-liner.

During one long pause, I thought of my dad. Several years earlier, we anxiously waited to see him at the hospital. I had wanted to make sure I got to talk to him in case it was for the last time. When we saw him, he was so calm and peaceful. He just smiled and spoke slowly and softly. He made a point to say who would get his toolbox.

I made a point to make eye contact and say out loud, "I love you," and then fought off the tears as our smiles connected.

He recovered.

Now, here I was. I knew I'd check out okay. I always did. But this was necessary. I had my kids to worry about. I felt Becky's warm soft hand squeeze love into me. I looked up, made a quip and she smiled, warming my heart. I apologized for going to work and minimizing my time at her side in the hospital after she gave birth to our children years ago.

Test results showed I was in no danger so I was left to rest. That's when serious activity picked up. The tempo went tilt. My room was needed for a real emergency. Nurses rolled me into the hallway and parked me against the wall. I was left in a semi-upright position. My wife wasn't with me. The doors flew open. An elderly lady was rushed inside the room I had just occupied. She was on life support. This was the real deal. It made me feel silly for being there in the first place. I wanted to get up and go but I was still linked to too many things I'd have to rip out. I didn't want that kind of attention so I just watched what was going on around me, like a fly on the wall. Nobody saw me, really, but I saw everything.

A family had gathered in seats outside the room from where the elderly lady was being treated. They were just across from me and down about 10 feet. They seemed alarmed but hopeful. Looking at them, I felt like the old lady would pull through. There were three generations. The hand-holding, praying family included the spouse of the old lady, her children and their high-school or college age daughters. I felt I shouldn't be there. I was invading their privacy. Just once did one of them look my way as if I revealed myself for a second and disappeared again.

I tried looking elsewhere but it was difficult. When the treatment room doors opened, the entire family leaned forward as one, hopeful. There was a millisecond of anticipation that loomed much longer than expected. Then, as I was drawn to the old man's face, I saw hope morph into hopelessness. He was devastated. His world crashed down and ended just then. He was in shock. He sat down, staring into thin air, silent. Then, his body shook violently and he sobbed heavily and loudly into his hands. I closed my eyes out of respect for the old man's privacy.

I had seen death before. I had seen heart-wrenched loved ones mourn. I had experienced

244

loss. But I had never experienced what this old man was experiencing – not even close.

Sometimes you know it is coming but sometimes you don't get to say goodbye at all.

Only in San Francisco!

It was early morning in Fisherman's Wharf. While waiting at a street corner, a strange sight grabbed our attention. A lady was walking backwards, ever so casually, at a pace somewhere between not too fast and not too slow.

I quickly reminded the kids, and myself, not to snicker when she neared. We missed the "walk" sign because although we faced it, we were concentrating on our peripheral vision. She passed us, backside first. Our eyes shifted to the other peripheral. Now we could see this lady's front side as she faced us walking away. She kept a steady pace, looking in our direction, totally without expression. And we looked in her direction, no longer coy, with wonderment written all over our faces. Straight-faced, she crossed a couple of streets as if she had eyes in the back of her head. We were mesmerized. How could she see where she was going? Why was she doing this? She seemed so at ease as if this was her daily routine. It probably was. We held a downright stare until she finally turned a corner. We looked away, scratched our heads and wondered out loud what the heck just happened.

Mixed in our visits to the usual tourist attractions – Alcatraz, Chinatown, wild sea lions at Pier 39, Little Italy and Lombard Street – we got in line to do that thing you feel you must do because you're in San Francisco, ride a trolley. We waited in the trolley line for a very long time. It was near the bay and chilly. The park next door had a lot of people chilling out. Then, I noticed a smell wafting in the air. It made me think back to my college days. So, we passed the time talking about hippies while we watched them dancing and singing around a man strumming an acoustic guitar.

Later in the afternoon, while resting in a park, I remembered a documentary – The Wild Parrots of Telegraph Hill. I convinced my family to walk up to COIT Tower on Telegraph Hill to go find this fascinating flock of wild parrots living there. It was a steep, long walk but we got there! By the way, the views of the street-laced hills were incredible. So, apparently was my lung capacity.

A group of college students were lying in the grass by COIT Tower. I approached them thinking they were locals and could direct me. As I stood over them, they casually looked up at me as if to say, what's up with this dude? That's when I asked where I could find the parrots flying around.

This awkward exchange made me think they might have had a hippie discussion of their own after I left, especially as I backpedaled away, not unlike the lady at the crosswalk.

Motel California

Desolate roads stretched into evening before we reached our destination just outside of Lava Beds

National Monument in northern California's inland no-man's land.

When I pre-booked this motel, our travel lady at AAA warned that it wasn't in their guide books at all. I had found it on the Internet and in my mapping of our trip I decided that this motel was all about location-location-location. There was nothing else around. Besides, the pictures looked decent enough. I was proud of my "find."

Had I known of any other accommodations or thought we could get away with sleeping under the stars, I would have pulled out of the parking lot as soon as we pulled into it. There was a strip of about six rooms encased in cinder block walls and a house across the way, a.k.a. lodge, hanging on from the 1930's, or so it seemed.

When I walked up to the "office" inside the old house, I was relieved the manager's name wasn't Norman Bates. I walked down a dim and eerily quiet hallway, drawn to a light like a bug. The light was emitting from a makeshift office. The live-in lady manager said she didn't think I was going to make it. It was getting late to check-in.

She kindly escorted me outside and over to the non-descript cinder block and motel room. I noticed she had an old metal, square, floor fan tucked under her arm. That was our "air conditioning." Inside were three beds, old carpet, cinder block walls and a bathroom occupied by a huge spider. The back window was unlocked. I promptly locked it. Later, I set a booby trap consisting of things that would fall over and make lots of noise if anyone came through it.

"Can you help me with your son's cot?" the nice lady asked.

I followed her to a nearby shed to retrieve a cot. This was after she offered the alternative, a mattress on the floor.

Had everything not appeared to be clean inside, we would have slept in the car for sure. But it was a long adventurous day and a bed was a bed ...or cot. On the other hand, there was no television or radio and no room key if you can believe that!

I mean, where ya gonna go, right?

Finally, after tucking the kids into "bed," I went outside with a plastic desk chair to sit on the concrete slab. I noticed that the door had eight holes that had been filled in. They looked to be about the size of bullet holes. Then, I tipped back on the chair and broke up the dead – and I mean DEAD – silence humming *Hotel California* by the Eagles.

Sports Parents

I have been both a youth sports coach and a parent of youths in sports. There are different coaching styles, different levels of skill and different parents.

My wife and I were watching our grade school son play in a flag football league. The year before, he had done well, standing out with some of his play. This year, he was getting lost in the pack. Only a few more games to go and the season would be over. The coach and assistant coach were buddies. Most of the plays went to the assistant coach's son. He was very good. My philosophy when I coached at this young level was to develop the kids by giving each some meaningful exposure to each position. Call it a difference in coaching philosophy. That said, I understood weighting things to tilt the outcome of games with winning in mind. It is fun to play but it's really fun to win. I got that.

My wife, Becky, is a very kind, patient, calm and understanding person. As we sat on the sideline she was talking under her breath about the obvious. I was content in riding things out and just accepting life is unfair, sometimes, but you move on. Then, my son was wide-open in the end-zone.

Another father grumbled, "Why didn't they throw it to him, he can catch."

Series after series, the plays mainly rotated with the assistant coach's son. He was good but others were good, too. On the sideline, I could hear more parents voicing their displeasure in watching a team live and die with one player. Becky's uncharacteristic grumbling raised the ante.

The action on the field was down by the far end zone. This was elementary school flag football so I didn't think it was a big deal to curve around the edge of the opposite end zone to bring a water bottle to my son, sitting out, while the line of lawn chair parents focused their attention in the other direction. When I got next to the assistant coach, I made a quiet but stern remark to him that it would be nice to rotate more meaningful touches of the ball to the other kids. He said he was in charge of rotations and it was fair. This insulted my intelligence because I knew the scheme they had going. Yes, each kid was put in each position and rotated around but the play-calling rotated with his son, mostly. If it was a pass, he was either the quarterback or primary receiver. If it was a run play, he was the running back. If he was anywhere else, he became the go-to receiver …most of the time.

I added words to the effect that, "No scouts are here. This should be about developing all of the kids for the next level, where at that point, it would be appropriate to feature the star player. But at this level, you are keeping potential other stars buried."

After huffing silently back to my lawn chair, I asked Becky if she could hear us. She said no and that besides, nobody was looking that way anyway.

We lost again!

That night I got an "earful" from the head coach in an e-mail about my bush-league behavior calling out his assistant coach in the middle of the game. I apologized for my timing but doubled-down on my point.

At the next game, I approached both men and said I was wrong to go about things the way I had and extended a handshake. This loosened things up and we chatted, chuckled and buried the hatchet with the consensus it was a learning experience for all and that good points were absorbed.

The next season, by the luck of the draw, we got the same coaching duo and "star" player. I didn't ask to switch teams and just went with it. At the first practice, we treated each other like old friends. It was a new start.

At the practice before the first game, the head coach said he would not be at the first game, neither would the assistant coach. They asked one father to be the fill-in head coach and gave him the playbook. They asked me to be his assistant. I agreed. They assured me I didn't need to prepare or do anything except show up and send kids in and out of the game.

I showed up but the fill-in head coach did not. It was a rude awakening. I was Johnny-on-the-spot. Conspiracy theories raced through my mind. I panicked and then, 15-minutes before kickoff, I grabbed the boys and took control. Fortunately, I had coached before, albeit baseball.

I need to give credit where credit is due; these boys were well coached and knew the plays.

Everything I called, worked wonderfully. The best part is I gave everyone a shot at being the featured running back and the featured receiver. Smiles were off the charts.

The assistant coach's son told me I wasn't doing things the way he was used to having them done. He also said he was used to getting the ball more. I knew it was a tough adjustment for him so I said the next two plays would be his.

We easily won. Parents lined up to say kind things to me because they knew it was a baptism by fire. I told parents and the assistant coach's wife that it had nothing to do with me and everything to do with the kids and how well the real coaches prepared them.

I never got thanks from the real coaches for filling in as head coach in a pinch. Nor did I mind. I didn't want them to feel I showed them up so I became mister volunteer parent for anything they needed for the rest of the season.

Before the last game, I had to fade back and handle a business cell phone call. The assistant coach had called me over with a shout and arm wave and I held a finger to say in a minute, phone in my other hand held to my ear. I had no responsibilities that game and plenty of other parents were there, plus the head coach, to give any needed assistance. Just before kickoff, I found the assistant coach's wife and handed her a donation for the coaches' gifts. I sat back, enjoyed the game and afterward, joined the team and parents in a pavilion for the end of season pizza party.

I shook the head coach's hand and congratulated him on doing a fine job and then extended my hand across the picnic table to the assistant coach offering the same. He didn't accept. All eyes were watching. I tried again. He said maybe later, his hands were dirty.

Attack of the Blood Thirsty Black Flies

Most of us couldn't stomach the ferry ride to Pelee Island. It was nighttime and Lake Erie was white capping. Grandma regretted her sugary snack and cup of coffee. Her eyes fixated at the bottom of a bag. The contents of her stomach followed. The boys returned from the bow, soaked head to toe.

The next day, we awoke at our beachfront rental to sunny skies and waves that were still pretty big. We swam, diving into the breaking waves all morning. Then, we noticed swimming companions peeking out from the water, shooting from waves, doing wild wrapping rituals on the beach. They were Lake Erie Water Snakes; an endangered species but you wouldn't have known that from looking around. Pelee Island was a haven for them.

That ended my swimming for the day, but the kids were having too much fun to care.

Pelee Island was perfect for bicycle riding an afternoon away so that's what we decided to do. Our destination was to be an old lighthouse built in 1834. Before we set out, we all took turns spraying each other with bug repellent.

"I swear they're biting me more after I put the repellent on than before," I complained to my wife, Becky. She said it was my imagination. Maybe it was.

It was time to go and Grandma, my mom, zoomed ahead. She lives life like she's forever 12.

"Why doesn't Grandma have to wear a bicycle helmet?" asked my 12-year-old daughter.

"Just ride," several of us sighed.

My niece was not very good at riding a bicycle, especially compared to her daredevil little brother. So, the pack broke in two. I kept pace with my daughter, son and nephew. My mom stayed back – much as she loved riding fast with a huge grin and wild eyes – with my niece, wife, sister and sister's boyfriend. About every quarter-mile, my niece wiped out. But the fractured pack kept moving down the road to an end of the island where we would eventually pick up a trailhead to a beach and finally the lighthouse.

I kept getting bit by black flies. No one else seemed to notice, so I gutted it out and continued. I really had no choice. It was more of a nuisance than anything else. Nearly two miles into the ride, there was a considerable gap between my group of kids and my niece's group of adults. I nearly jackknifed my bike I was bit so damn hard by a black fly. It hurt but that pain was quickly eclipsed by another, and another and another.

I was miserable.

It turned out that I was no longer the only one. My daughter and nephew were ahead of my son and me. They slowed down because the black flies grew thicker and thicker. The four of us pressed on a little bit further, hoping we'd blow through the swarm. By the time we reached the end of the road and the beginning of the trailhead, we were engulfed in a cloud of black flies. My daughter was hurting out loud, my son had no filter as he shrieked from the constant biting, and my little nephew suffered in silence. I yelled at the flies. It was all I could do before we turned around and tried to flee. My daughter was the fastest out of there. I hung back with the two young boys. They needed to keep both hands on their handlebars and that kept them from swatting at the meat-eating flies. The swarm was so thick, and the bites so ferocious, my son was bleeding. I considered maybe it was my scent since I had attracted them long before anyone else even noticed. I told the boys to ride ahead and follow my daughter.

Once they were well ahead of me, I rode like the wind in my effort to escape the misery. But misery was glued to me. As it turned out, the flies never left the boys, either, nor my daughter for that matter. When the four of us flew past the slower-paced riders, headed in the opposite direction, the kids were screaming in pain – except for my silent nephew – from the constant biting. As the slower group described to us later, when we flew past them our white shirts looked black, and we

254

resembled a bad Pig-Pen scene from the Peanuts comic strip. As for me, they reported that I looked just like a bee-keeper blanketed in bees. The black cloud stuck to me no matter where I went. As I rode past the slower group, I yelled to turn around but it was too late. The flies swarmed them, too, unbeknownst to me because I had the boys to worry about. My daughter was too far ahead for me to have any immediate concern.

It was sheer terror for about two miles. At some point, my wife left her slower group and caught up to us, typical of a mother needing to protect her young.

I had to make the painful decision to have the boys stop their bicycles a couple of times to shake and swat the flies away.

After a while, I said, "Just ride! The only way this is going to stop is getting back to the house."

It was awful not being able to help them. Both boys were downright scared. My son yelled out loud. My nephew had horror in his eyes but never said a peep. They both rode and rode because there was no alternative. They looked to me for help but there was nothing I could do except emphasize that the only way to make it stop was to get back so ride-ride-ride!

Finally, we got back, shook the flies off and ran inside to safety. I went back outside to look down the road to see how far back the others were. That's when my sister skid across the lawn, jumped from her bike before it stopped and sped off in her car. It happened in a blur.

Because my niece couldn't ride a bike far under normal conditions, she was being eaten alive along with everyone in her group. She was in hysterics by the time the rescue vehicle brought her back.

An hour later, small amounts of blood were wiped from the fair-skinned youngsters. Tears dried and medicine applied, we sat around the room overlooking the beach and lake, completely drained from the experience.

My niece joined us. She was washed up and wrapped in a towel for comfort.

Since I wasn't with her on the ride, I said, "Tell me about your awesome bike ride."

Her bottom lip puffed out as she softly replied, "I fell down a hill, got scraped and got eaten by flies."

"So it was fun," I teased.

"No," she said sheepishly.

"Was it kind of fun?" Grandma asked.

She looked through sad eyes with that puffy lip expression and faintly said, "Yes."

The room erupted in laughter because we all knew this was an incredible experience we'd not soon forget.

Dead Bolt

I was exhausted as I stepped onto the elevator to go to the second floor. Elevator to the second floor, ridiculous, I know.

The doors opened. The convenience of seeing my room right off the elevator lobby made me crack a smile just as an elderly woman passed with a bucket of ice. Her smile back made me uncomfortable.

Sliding my keycard to get the green light to enter, I fumbled everything. Three hands were needed. The little light turned red just as I cranked the locked handle up – only it didn't go up. On my second try it worked so I quickly used my butt to wedge the door open enough to transfer my baggage from inches outside of the room to inches inside it.

Once on the inside, I kicked my stuff to the side just enough to close the door. I flipped the deadbolt but it froze just shy of locking. I was too tired to complain. I swung the chain lock over and leaned an ironing board against the door to sound an alarm …just in case. I was out like a light.

My eyes snapped open from a sound sleep as I sprang from the bed. The door had been breached. The penetrating sound of the ruptured chain lock combined with the crashing ironing board shot an overdose of alarm through my previously comatose body.

I gustily yelled some intimidating "stuff" – Oh yah, I have pipes – at the scoundrel breaking into my room.

Then, I flung open the door – thinking maybe I should have stopped at the peep hole – to catch a glimpse of the burglar bolting through the door leading to the staircase beyond the elevator.

I called the front desk only to find out, according to the clerk, that this dude was a regular and always got this room so she absent-mindedly gave him a key.

Unbelievable!

But I believed her incompetency excuse. There was fear in her voice of losing a much needed job as she rattled off the name and number of her manager and next of kin.

I'm not the snitching type so I forgave her and said, "No worries."

The clerk's ramblings described this dude as being more than freaked out by the encounter.

As I sat down, I laughed my ass off at what had just happened, thinking of the buzz kill I must have served the guy looking to crash in my room.

It could have been worse. What if I awoke to him sliding in bed with me? Now, that would have been a "dead bolt!"

Vanity

I hadn't been to a high school reunion since the tenth. But I planned to go to my 25th. And as it approached, I got ready.

Teeth whitening – check!

Lose weight – check!

Sun tan – check!

Haircut – check!

New clothes – check!

"You're worse than a woman," said my wife, Becky – easy coming from someone who wakes up looking great.

In my "makeover" for the class reunion, I stopped using my tooth whitener from the dentist. It was making my gums hurt. Well, one more treatment for good measure, despite the deep sharp pain. Then, I was done. My workout routine went from grueling to tilt! On the last day before we traveled, I biked, ran and rowed the whole day away. Then, I went to the pool and swam. I remember that my system was experiencing some sort of shock. After all, my internal temperature was at an all-time high, it was a very hot and humid afternoon and that water was ice cold. I swam, laid in the hot sun, swam some more, opening my eyes underwater. That night, my body temperature was still boiling so I put the fan on high and positioned it right at me.

Ahhhhh. I was ready.

I woke up with a weird sensation on the right side of my face. I figured I slept wrong and it would go away.

On the long drive to the ole hometown, my face felt a little weirder instead of better. I asked Becky if I looked okay.

"You look fine."

I don't even think her eyes left her smart phone.

We arrived in town and got ready. There was a pre-reunion party and more people were rumored to be attending that than the actual reunion planned for the following day.

"My face doesn't feel right," I told my wife.

"Oh honey, what happened?" she was looking at me now and not liking what she saw.

The right side of my face was not working. I had a crooked smile because half of it was limp. I brushed it off as some anomaly that would pass. Becky was more concerned than I so I tried to lighten the mood by doing Elvis Presley impersonations. Something about my crooked smile, deepened voice and using the word, "baby" made her burst into tears …with laughter.

On to the pre-reunion.

259

It was really nice to see so many old friendly faces. My two best friends weren't at this reunion due to vacation and work travel. So, I mingled.

I could definitely feel my face gradually getting worse. I drank some beer so I wouldn't be as self-conscious. Regardless, I thought a couple of people gave me funny looks. Maybe I was paranoid. In the middle of a conversation, a moment called for laughter.

A girl said, "You have a really cute crooked smile. I don't remember you having a crooked smile."

Another drink didn't drown that last comment so Becky and I left – and eventually landed in the Emergency Room.

A day and a half dozen tests later, they ruled out stroke and said I had Bell's Palsy. By this time, half of my face was completely paralyzed and wouldn't recover for months.

I walked out of there with one eye taped closed because I couldn't blink. Half of my face drooped off of my jaw bone. Still, I was thinking I probably looked good enough to make the end of the reunion.

But my car mirror said, no.

Walk of Shame

Long before 9-11, terrorism was in my consciousness. When I was overseas, posters of the most wanted terrorists were prominently hung in our barracks. Those of us who drove were taught to examine the underside of vehicles for bombs.

Once, I had to fly out of Frankfurt, Germany to the U.S. on the Fourth of July. Just prior to my trip, a broadcast warned of a terrorist threat planned for July on just such a flight. I remember expecting a boom the entire trip – and it was a long one – over the Atlantic Ocean to New York.

With that backdrop and the world we live in today, I can understand the precautions that are necessary when we use airports, government buildings, and other public places. Sometimes, I complain about the loss of freedom but I'm really complaining about my personal inconvenience.

On one of our family vacations, we stayed at the same hotel where, just outside, a sniper's bullet almost killed President Reagan. We woke early to get a head start on a busy day. We had a pre-scheduled tour of the Capitol Building, located at the far end of The National Mall in Washington D.C. This would kick off a full day of walking through the Mall and visiting many of the monuments. Heat was definitely going to be a problem. In recent days, the temperature had been in triple digits, and more of the same was expected. So, like a good Boy Scout, I was going to be prepared and filled up my camel pack (a small backpack that only holds water). Then I filled plastic bottles to go inside my wife's and kids' backpacks. Since we'd be on the go all day and well into the evening, I also threw in a fist full of snacks consisting of granola, crackers and trail mix.

My wife mentioned something about restrictions and security checkpoint at the Capitol Building. I blew it off. I mean c'mon – it was going to be a hundred degrees! We only had water and snacks.

Open the packs, take a look, let us through. There was no doubt in my mind that that would be the extent of it. It's not like we live in Russia (my mind sometimes sticks in the 1980s).

"Subway?" My wife suggested.

"Let's hoof it. It doesn't look so bad," I said glancing at a map.

I definitely underestimated the time it would take, something I am not known to do.

"Look kids, White House," snap-snap and we had our pic to show we were there. Then we were gone.

Once we were on The Mall, we ran in spurts in order to meet our time slot for our scheduled tour. The length of the Mall was grossly underestimated.

"Damn map maker," I muddled.

My wife didn't let it slide. I was to blame. Little did she know, I was just warming up.

We joined the line, which was already snaking outside, and waited. It was getting hot outside.

The kids asked for water and I said, "No, we need to conserve it."

You know kids, no foresight. They would deplete our water supply by the time we got inside and then complain they needed a bathroom. That was my thinking anyway.

Every now and then as tourists entered into the building, we noticed they were sent back out to dispose of things not approved for entry.

"We should dump out our water," my wife said.

I looked at her like she was crazy, "Are you kidding me – it's going to be a hundred today. It's water!"

When we finally entered the building, there were scanners and commotion everywhere. We had to remove bags, belts, shoes, you-name-it, for inspection.

"This can't go in," said security.

I was directed to take my camel pack outside to pour it out and return. A guard at the door would let me in and out. But I wasn't permitted to dump water just outside the door. I had to go into the grass off to the side of the long line of people waiting to get inside. They looked at me like I looked at others coming back out earlier. As I poured, I saw some couples exchange words resulting in either water being dumped or a shake of a head, no.

When I got back inside, my wife was smiling and security was frowning.

"This has to go, too," security said, handing me a bowl full of snacks.

I made a basket out of the front of my shirt, dumped in what I considered lunch to save a few bucks and headed back outside. This time, I was directed to the other side of the line where the dumpsters were located. I felt self-conscious on this walk of shame.

Back inside, my wife and security guard were both frowning. Now I had to go dump the water bottles. I could have kicked myself for not thinking to dump them when I dumped the camel pack. As I poured away hydration in the greenest grass I had ever seen in July, I couldn't even bear to look at the crowd of people who certainly recognized me by now.

A guard at the door smiled out of familiarity when I re-entered.

My wife and son were standing in the clear on the other side of the metal detectors. It struck me as a little off that my daughter was still on my side so I nudged her forward, anxious to put this freak-show behind us.

"Hold up!" came a voice I was growing to despise.

"Gotta take it out," I was told.

"Really?" I gave a look of c'mon!

I didn't mind the three shame walks because it was my fault for trying to get over. But they got me on all my goods. Yes, I was an idiot for thinking I was sensible. What could possibly be the hold-up this time, I wondered. Security pulled out sun screen from the bottom of my daughter's back pack.

"The dumpster is just over there, outside the doors," I directed my teen daughter.

She looked startled. I had rattled her from her comfort zone. I was sacrificing my flesh and blood so that I could avoid a fourth strut down shame alley. Reluctantly, she complied. The doors and wall were glass so I could watch her the entire way.

Meanwhile, my wife and son were shooed off to keep the throngs of people flowing.

Commands echoed, directing us and others, "Clear the area, keep it moving."

"We'll catch up inside," I called out to my wife as she and our son disappeared from sight.

"You too, sir," said security putting a hand on me, pushing but not shoving.

I stood pat and explained, "I have to wait for my daughter, she'll be right back. She had to dump something outside."

"Doesn't matter, you have to move on," he said pushing against me again.

I understood rules and why water and crackers had to be thrown out to keep large crowds from being bogged down by deeper inspection. It was easier and efficient this way, especially considering it was the Capitol Building. But there was no way I was leaving my 13-year-old girl to fend for herself in that crowd.

"She'll be here in a second, sir," I said with a pleading smile.

As he started to repeat himself, my look changed. Something about it made the guard step to the side as if I had complied and wasn't there anymore.

I felt terrible for wimping out on a fourth trip outside, but I was so familiar with the surroundings by then, I had convinced myself that my daughter would be just fine. Standing there was the most shame I felt. Although each second seemed like a minute, my daughter was by my side again and we entered the U.S. Capitol Building, safe and sound.

The Supreme Court may ponder whether they are an equal branch of government because by the time we entered that building, we had replenished our water supply, compliments of a drinking fountain. Security looked at everything we had and let us through without having to dump anything.

Suburban Standoff

With my house located near the top of a hill, I noticed that cars tended to go over the speed limit coming down our street and sounded even louder going up it. This never concerned me until I had kids walking without the benefit of sidewalks to and from the school bus stop.

One of my neighbors had been at war with speeders for quite a while. He had even posted a homemade wooden speed limit sign in his front yard. It wasn't long before someone spray painted some additional words on it. He was later required to remove it. Up went one of those speed monitoring machines. The kind in which some people like to ring up a high score since there's no consequence, just showing you how fast, or slow, you're going.

My barking at motorists began after one almost killed my kids and me. The driver hit a slick spot speeding downhill after a winter storm and sailed across the road to our side as we walked up. We had no time to react. I instinctively put my body between the truck and my kids. It was all I could do. Fortunately, the driver recovered and turned away just arm's reach from me. I also had to deal with the lady who sailed down the road every morning in a minivan doing speeds nobody else ever approached. She had to exceed 50 miles per hour or more. Our limit is 25 miles per hour. I jumped out in the road and made my point clear. She drove like an old lady after that. On Halloween night, a teenager drove up the road recklessly, with no regard for the children who were out trick-ortreating. I stood in front of the fast approaching car, hearing the gasps of those around until he stopped. I'm stupid that way. When I went to his side window, he sped off. Numerous mailbox mishaps and other accidents have occurred over time. Many neighbors have called the police but as you can imagine, these reports are a dime a dozen in suburbia. So, the speed machine shows up again.

Over time, you succumb to the facts of life. People are going to speed. People are going to eat bagels, apply lipstick or text on phones while they drive. I stopped consciously caring.

One morning, I was chatting with another neighbor on the street. He was watering flowers at the foot of his driveway and I was retrieving the morning paper. I joined him in his driveway for a friendly conversation. We marveled at the gorgeous weather. A car approached so fast, it was clear it was speeding.

As I took a precautionary step away from the curb, I motioned down with my hands as if to say, "slow down."

He slowed down all right. He came to a sudden and complete stop.

I was no rookie to conflict so I came over to his car door to hear what he had to say. He delivered a mouthful. I blamed him for speeding. He didn't like the accusation. It was hard to believe I alone had put him in this mood but I was certainly his outlet.

"You know what …" he said in anger, opening his door to get out in an act of intimidation.

I didn't intimidate easily so I stepped in, closer, instead of away as he must have expected me to do. So we stood facing each other. His hesitation meant this was not going to escalate to fisticuffs. I had that much experience so I remained calm, stood my ground but allowed him an out. He argued I had it wrong. He said something about having kids of his own as if it proved his innocence.

I simply repeated, "You were speeding."

I never resorted to shouting, although I maintained an assertive voice. I never used bad language, name calling or anything else to incite him further; typical mistakes made by people in the heat of the moment which inevitably make a contained situation spiral out of control. But I was not relenting on the fact he was speeding. That much was clear.

Frustrated, he jumped back in his car and said, "Then call the cops!" and he drove away.

I waived through the few cars backed up behind my suburban foe. Each driver had an alarmed look as they passed. I crossed the road back to my retired friend, who was still idly hosing down his plants.

"I had your back if he took a swing at you," he said, seriously. "I do what you did all the time and nobody has ever gotten out of their car like that."

Later, on a walk with my wife and dog, I could swear it was the errant driver approaching from the opposite direction, jogging. As we passed each other, we both chuckled and smiled like the middle-aged dads we were, finding humor or embarrassment in our earlier suburban standoff.

SOME CLOSING THOUGHTS

The experiences I've shared are only a part of my story. With all of my experiences mingling with the many backgrounds of people cited in, "About the Author," I have gained some thoughts and philosophies that may not be embraced by many. Any similarity in my thoughts expressed in this section to what others' may have written is unintentional.

~

Sometimes we lose sight of what's truly important to us. But when it's rediscovered we're liberated – for a moment anyway.

~

There are two sides to the mirror. The side you see and the side you don't.

~

For every cause, there's someone willing to lie for the "greater good."

~

Don't judge others. You didn't walk their path. Had you, your eyes may see as theirs do.

~

You see only that which you want to see. If you disapprove and want to change somebody, simply choose to see them in a new and good way and so that is how they will now appear to you.

~

Life is how you take it and what you make of it.

~

The weak are aggressive. The strong are not.

~

The secret to happiness is seeing life as a great adventure – nothing big, just discovering wonderment in the overlooked. When sorrow seeps in, it is only to remind you of the good times before

and after. So, embrace it, for without it you
wouldn't know happiness.

~

When I was a boy, I had fun with everyone.
When I was a teen, some turned on me.
When I became a man, I turned on some.
Now, I'm a boy again.

~

Building blocks make for shortcuts to thinking. The
past builds the future. So the future is self-fulfilling
until one day things don't add up. That's when you
realize one of your building blocks turned you into
an idiot. That is, if you're smart.

~

The world is so complex, it's simple.
Happiness is simplicity.

~

Who are they competing against if you're no longer competing? And is there a winner?

~

Some pound their chest.
They need to be superior.
Some scream in your ear.
They need to be heard.

Some pretend not to notice.
Some pretend not to hear.

Some don't pretend.

~

What is a man?
Someone who doesn't need to prove they are one.

~

Vengeance.
No thank you.

Smile and be happy.
That'll kill 'em!

~

Beauty is seeing the miracle in the plain.

~

Life. It is taken for granted most of the time until it is seen as incredibly delicate. Fear makes it delicate. Don't be fearful or you won't live.

~

What happens after death? Eternity. But what does that mean?

~

I go through life seeing what I see.
But there is so much more that I miss.
How do I know?

I am who I am.
And I strive to be who I want.
Others see who I am, why not me?

I am what I was and became what I sought.

I see who I am, but why can't they?

~

Look and you shall find.
Don't look and you shall see.

~

We are often presented with two sides to a story but we have learned to say there are really three. There's the side you agree with and the side you don't. When both are presented we claim objectivity. When one is favored, it is said to be biased. Our experiences add to bias. Some cannot see beyond their own experience. But the unbiased truth is in the third, untold ...story. And it doesn't pit the two sides against each other.

~

Objecting to an established norm and creating your own way does not mean you are wrong or rebelling, just acknowledging what is best for you, not what society tells you what is best for you. That said, mistakes happen, but that doesn't mean you are being punished or were stupid. Sometimes the difference between success and failure is not with the whole, but just a part. Rethink and try again.

~

We are limited to the minds we surround ourselves with. Expand your circles of influence, and better choices result. Sometimes choices present themselves where you previously saw none. Listen to others who have had a different journey than yours. Instead of judging the differences negatively, try to understand a world in which you have not lived, and you may find tolerance or acceptance.

~

You may define me by a mere part of what I am. But the whole of me includes many parts. To know me is to love me. If you don't love me, you are focusing too much on a small part of me. And that part of me is likely also a part of you.

~

An award winning filmmaker leaves most of his work on the cutting room floor, usually because it's crap. But he doesn't let the bulk of his work define

him. He is defined by the little bit of his work that
turns out to be exceptional.

~

They Laugh

They laugh behind my back,
But I still smile and give the greeting of the day.

Why are they threatened by me?
I'd don't mean them any harm.

Please don't envy what I am or what I have,
It's really no more than you.

Except for one thing –

I wish you my strength,
So that you, too, find happiness.

~

Ripples
Sea formed me – I splashed – And became the sea

Human-kind struggles with self-absorption. We
want to live forever. Then we want life after death.
But no matter what awaits in afterlife, we live on.

After all, matter and energy cannot be destroyed or created, and there is no end or beginning to time and space. We are eternal.

The universe is in perfect harmony. Good cannot exist without evil. Everything connects. That is our destiny. A drop in a pool of water sends ripples to its furthest shore despite the obstacles.

We may just be drops in a sea but without drops, a sea does not exist. Subtle splashes ripple forever in calm waters. Thunderous splashes may go unnoticed in stormy waters.

We are mostly water; without it we die. After we splash, what is the ripple-effect?

~

Finding My Way by Knowing My Place

I grew up a humble son,
appreciating everything we had.

My heart poured empathy for others,
and optimism flowed through my veins.

I was no greater than any,
nor were any greater than me.

I never forgot my roots,
but at times I branched away.

I never understood those of greed.
Why are they not humble like me?

So I rose up to humble the brazen ones.

I was no longer humble,
and they could not be won.

I will die a humble man.
Happy.

~

Who Am I, Really?

I am what my parents rebelled against. I am what
my parents cherished.

I am a culture. I am a counter-culture.

I am a generation. I am every generation.

I am a moment in time. I am a body of work.

I am an encounter that changed me. I am many
encounters that never changed me.

I am the words someone shared to help me see. I
am the words I wish someone shared.

I am what I hate. I am what I love.

I am a label. I am what I cannot label.

I am to one group what I am not to another.

I am to the memory of some what I am not in the present to others.

I am evolving. I am also parts unchanged.

I am like anyone else. I am unique.

I am a hero. I am a villain.

I am my imagination. I am others' imaginations.

I am your mirror.

~

Gaining Faith by Losing Religion

Science shows that it all came from one point of origin as if someone just snapped their fingers and said, "Let there be life." And so there was. Yet most of what is around us is not even detected by us. We define it as dark matter and dark energy but it isn't dark at all.

The universe and everything we know lives by codes and are mathematically defined. It's not random. How did this design come into existence?

If matter and energy cannot be destroyed or created, and there is no end or beginning to time and space, everything is eternal.

Why does evolution need to prove or disprove anything? Perhaps life here was born from a seed that grew into different things much like the universe itself. Who planted the seed? At what point was man as we know him created? Perhaps it's as DNA and the human genome point out – East Africa a long time ago. And like the Universe, like life on Earth, Man multiplied and spread.

Our original parents on the Homo sapiens family tree may have been told the truth of our creation, what is expected of us and what will happen to us. So those who stayed in Africa and those who ventured from Africa had with them an oral story to be passed down.

Have you ever sat around a table and listened to members of the same family with the same experience describe it differently and debate what really happened? For goodness sakes, they were all there. Yet they recall it differently – and with great passion.

Perhaps we are all imperfect children recalling the original story inaccurately. Yet there are many common threads to these stories. Whether it is the followers of Jesus Christ, Allah, Buddha, Native Americans or African tribal lore and faiths, we are all touched by God – even those that don't believe in God follow many common beliefs as well.

There is no mistaking that man feels good about himself when he performs kind gestures and helps others. It has a positive impact on the mind and body. It's a fact.

But we struggle daily with the other side too – greed.

Why do we fight amongst ourselves differentiating and alienating each other based on the differences we observe? Physically, we are said to be virtually identical no matter our race or sex yet we have prejudices. And so it is spiritually too.

I may find salvation through MY lord Jesus Christ. This is because it is the story my member at the family table tells because that is how they remember seeing or hearing the truth. But a brother or sister at that table may have the same savior but by a different name or perhaps no name at all.

Why can't we all be right and wrong? If you are agnostic and practice a wholesome life, why can't you be judged by our God for your conduct? Who am I to condemn you?

It is the non-loving side of what we are that is greedy and begins to judge and rule and create dividing lines between "us" and "them." To win our battles we bear false witness, we lie, cheat, steal and even kill. We see it in politics, religion, race, sexual orientation, social class, education, status and in everything we seek to define ourselves.

If we can look beyond intolerance, we can embrace the universal belief system we share and apply it to all walks of life, not just to those who walk like "us" – "Do onto others as you would wish them do onto you." In my religion, it is known as "The Golden Rule." And when practiced with every living thing you encounter, this simple rule can move mountains.

~

In closing,

I am thankful for ...

Parents who loved me so much that I grew up knowing no fear.

Friends who taught me which boundaries should or shouldn't be explored.

A sister to experience laughter and conflict, sometimes within seconds.

My hometown for lessons on change.

An extended family that opened my eyes to diversity and respect for all.

The U.S. Army for introducing me to so many cultures.

College for balancing seriousness with immaturity.

The beginning of my career to learn what I did and didn't want to be for the rest of it.

My wife for believing in what I can do and encouraging me to make dreams come true.

Naysayers and pessimists who fuel me to achieve what they cannot.

My children for teaching me as much about life as I teach them.

All that is good and bad for shaping me into someone I am proud to be.

If you made it here,

THANK YOU!

About the Author:

I try to balance responsibility with irresponsibility because too much of either will ruin you.

Perhaps I have a unique perspective. Why do I think I have a unique perspective? Because it's difficult to find people who share my views. I have been exposed to so much from so many viewpoints. And I took it all in.

A country boy knows rural life. A city boy knows the streets. A rich kid knows wealth. A suburbanite knows middleclass. A traveler knows other cultures. I know many walks of life, personally and intimately.

My parents both came from large families in Cleveland. I spent many weekends per year for nearly two decades with these families in these homes, roaming these neighborhoods, learning. My parents left the city and moved to Avon Lake ahead of the highway. It was here that they raised me and my sister. I lived in what was a farm town, exploring endless woodland adventures, daily. But this rural wonderland transformed as I grew and it slowly turned into an affluent suburb. My dad rose from poverty and my mom from working class roots to achieve the comforts of middle-class suburbia. I had friends that were poorer and richer than me. I spent time with the wealthy and those living paycheck to paycheck. I saw vastly different lifestyles on a regular basis. I ate at their tables. I listened to their stories. I understood what made them, them, and observed how they think.

I worked at a country club and spent 4-8 hours per day listening to the über-wealthy and how they think and behave. I delivered newspapers in a tough neighborhood where many of my small town's hoodlums came from. I had fought people who ended up in prison or dead. In high school, youthful mischief had more serious consequences and I found myself in more than my share of trouble.

Then, I enlisted in the U.S. Army. In the service, I volunteered to go overseas so I could tour Europe. And that's what I did with a lot of my free time for about three years. I was stationed at a NATO base. I learned the cultures of several countries. I ate at the tables of Brits and Dutch. I listened to their stories. I observed their traditions. I knew them well.

I went off the beaten path to experience Germany, France, Holland, Belgium, Switzerland, Austria and Italy. I talked at length to people I'd meet from shop keepers to those my age. I befriended an Italian and asked him why so many people in Italy don't look Italian. He laughed and said I watched too many American movies.

My closest friends in the Army provided me an education on life, too. I spent a few years knowing many a tale from the bayou of Louisiana, the reservations of Native Americans, the Bronx, L.A., Florida, Maine and Alaska just to name some. Oh, and according to some, I was so cool, I should be black. I ate their foods and practiced their family traditions. After all, we lived together and were a family. Some of us remain close to this day. So it goes.

I learned to respect differences and even embrace them. I come from a background that had its share of trials and tribulations. I was sometimes the target of verbal and physical attacks. I learned how to defend myself on these accounts. In doing so, I picked up on what makes people the way they are, and how to handle them. The latter is sometimes a work-in-progress. Through childhood, U.S. Army, college, early career, self-employment, marriage and fatherhood, I also learned – and continue to learn – much about myself.

I have an open mind. I don't see limitations. I see possibility. In short, I think deeply, laugh openly and try to be kind. And I somehow find adventure, often in the ordinary.

Oh, I also run OhioTraveler.com.

Made in the USA
Lexington, KY
04 January 2017